Neng Da:
The Super Punches

Neng Da:
The Super Punches

by
Master Hei Long

Turtle Press   Hartford

To contact the author or order additional copies of this book:
Turtle Press
403 Silas Deane Hwy.
PO Box 290206
Wethersfield, CT 06129-0206
1-800-778-8785
www.turtlepress.com

Cover Illustration by Ken Cotrona
Interior Illustrations by Master Hei Long

ISBN   1-880336-13-8
First Edition

NOTE TO READERS

Consult a physician before undertaking this or any other exercise regimen. The skills presented in this book are for information purposes only.   Neither the author nor the publisher assumes any responsibility for the use or misuse of the information contained in this book.

Contents

Introduction

Neng Da, which translated literally means The Super Punches is a study of primary and supplemental power sources for hand strikes. The work is intended to be a tool for achieving optimum striking force in a number of punches, sutos, palms and backhands, based on the principles of   compound power movements and centrifugal force. Unlike many studies in the field of self-defense, Neng Da transcends the theoretical, goes beyond oversimplified loyalty to form and style. It approaches the learning process from practical, logical premises relying on the science of physics which encompasses those laws of nature that frame our physical capabilities by the sum of our knowledge and understanding of how our bodies are capable of moving. Science, specifically the laws of nature, is at the very root of all that we study in the martial arts, and therefore a return to those principles to enhance the efficiency of our most crucial tools, our striking weapons, is a much needed study.

Though we teach avoidance of confrontations and the application of   minimal force to stop an aggressor, it is overly presumptive to assume that even a best effort will be sufficient to stop any opponent we may encounter, and in reality, too many students appear far more effective during training than they really are. An opponent who is really trying to hurt you is far more difficult to stop than a training partner. Consequently, the practitioner who is unable to inflict damage with hand strikes and kicks may be found powerless to stop a relentless aggressor. A companion volume to this work, Neng Tai, will study maximizing kicking power. Here we will focus strictly on hand strikes.

Chapters One and Two, which are introductory in nature, study primary, compound and centrifugal force power sources as well as the five basic movements which provide the foundation for the movements in the following four chapters. Chapters Three through Six are the application chapters which utilize the principles of the first two chapters in various hand strike movements. Overall you should find Neng Da to provide a practical learning process to enhance the total impact force of your hand strikes thus increasing your ability and effectiveness as a self-defense practitioner.

Chapter One:
Generating Impact Power

The final definition of *Impact Power*, what it means in terms of cause and effect in relation to martial arts, is what results are achieved from a striking effort. In this chapter, we will be studying the sources of striking power from the physical perspective: i.e., how to transfer motion into striking force. We will be looking at primary, multiple, and centrifugal force patterns attempting to understand their nature and design; but like all serious sciences: theories, hypotheses, and studies in the martial arts always leave latitude for a deeper and more profound analysis of detail. The zeal to achieve perfection is what motivates the entrepreneur to a greater level of knowledge and skill. The body's only limitation is that which is imposed upon it by the mind. Therefore, the greater the understanding, the greater the capacity for skill. To that end, we are going to be stretching - not the body, but the mind.

Part One: Compound Power Movements

Look at *Graph A*. There are twenty-four governing and interdependent factors listed which have an effect on the total impact force of your strikes. The circular, center pattern in which the graph is presented has not been chosen to be appealing to the eye: the circle represents continuity. Cast off just one factor and that continuity is broken; effectiveness is diminished; total impact force is compromised.

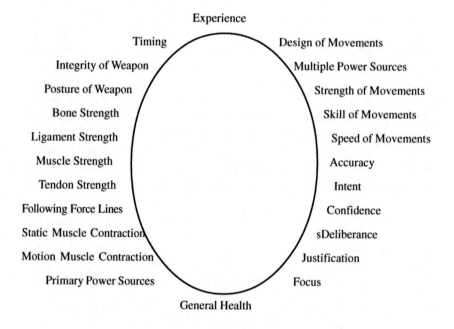

Graph A: Total Impact Force

Beginning at the top of Graph A and moving clockwise:

Experience: There is no substitute for experience. The more familiar you are with a movement, the more easily it will flow, minimizing exertion in performance.

Design of Movements: All movements in martial arts follow a tried and proven design. Once you have made whatever modifications are appropriate for your body type, follow and practice those movements progressively to maximize efficiency.

Multiple Power Sources: This concept, as you will see in this chapter, is synonymous with depressing the accelerator in an automobile: increasing the power source increases the output.

Strength, Skill, Speed, and Accuracy of movements come from specified training, and result in irresistible defensive and offensive technique. Each is trained separately, then combined in the performance of movements.

Intent is being predisposed, beforehand, to fight your best or not at all.

Confidence comes from training and experience. It is knowing you are prepared and skillful in defending yourself.

Deliberance: Techniques, properly executed and successful, are not incidental. They are designed for effectiveness. Therefore, the effort is a deliberate, confident one.

Justification is knowing you are right, not restraining yourself or your output for lack of feeling justified in your efforts.

Focus: This is your concentration; not allowing yourself to be distracted from your efforts.

General Health: An injured, infirm, or generally unhealthy body is incapable of maximum performance. Caring for your general health is therefore crucial to your abilities.

Primary Power Sources: Progressive training demands that basic movements reach an appropriate skill level before adding more technical, complicated movements.

Motion Muscle Contraction: It is important to know and properly utilize the correct muscles to initiate and follow movements to their points of completion.

Static Muscle Contraction: It is of equal importance to know and properly flex corresponding muscles to solidify joint positions to resist negative impact force.

Following Force Lines: It is important to adhere to the specifics of the lines of drive in executing strikes to achieve optimum efficiency and effectiveness.

Tendon Strength: Tendon strength is built through repetition of movements with resistance, and is required to alleviate or at least reduce the incidence of muscle injury.

Muscle Strength: Muscle moves bone. The greater the strength of skeletal muscles, the greater the potential for power.

Ligament Strength: Ligaments tie bones to bones forming joints. A weakened joint, due to weak ligaments, will make high impact strikes painful to the individual delivering them.

Bone Strength: Of course, strong muscles, tendons and ligaments will be neutralized by weak bones as well as muscles and connective tissues.

Posture of Weapon: Improperly formed anatomical weapons are a disaster waiting for a time and place to occur. Sprains are a very common result of improperly formed weapons.

Integrity of Weapon: The colliding forces of weapon meeting target will become increasingly greater as your strength and skill increase. There will come a time when it will become necessary for you to develop your anatomical weapons. This process was taught in detail in the book, *Iron Hand of the Dragon's Touch.*

Timing is the synchronization of all movements used in a specific technique and is a major key to optimizing power.

All of these factors contribute to the final product of Impact Force. Some are design factors, some deal with the laws of physics, some are related to physical conditioning, and some are psychological factors. All of them play an equally important role in the ultimate goal of perfection and maximizing power.

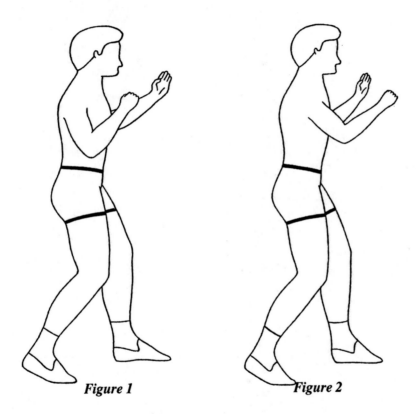

Figure 1   *Figure 2*

Observe Figures 1 through 3. In Figure 1, you are positioned in a typical ready stance and will be throwing a short, straight-line punch with the right hand. In Figure 2, the punch is half extended toward your target. At this height, your target would be the heart or sternum.

15

Figure 4

Figure 3

In Figure 3, the punch is fully locked into the open position. This is a simple, short, straight-line punch.

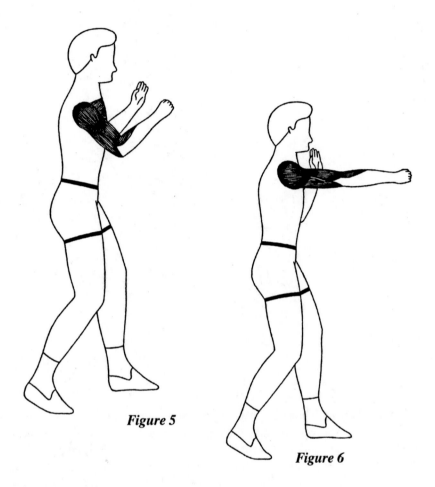

Figure 5

Figure 6

The movement is powered by motion contraction of the right pectoralis muscles[1], motion contraction of the right deltoid, and motion contraction of the triceps group. Static contraction will occur in all of the muscles of the forearm and hand, the biceps, latissimus dorsi, and all of the posture group[2]. The motion contraction group is illustrated in Figures 4 through 6.

[1] The Pectoralis Major and Minor are involved in raising the Humerus, the bone of the upper arm.
[2] The posture group is the Spinal Erectors, Rhomboids, Abdominals, and the leg muscles.

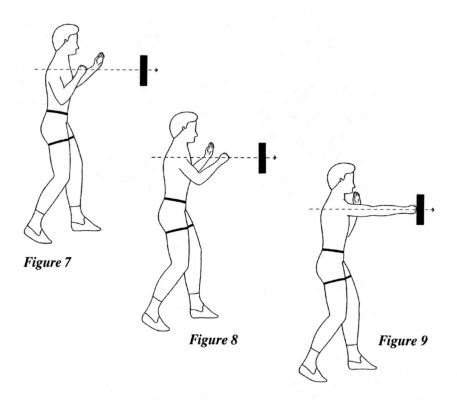

Figure 7

Figure 8

Figure 9

In Figures 7 through 9, we're going to follow the line of drive for the straight-line punch and study the related movements. Timed muscle exertion over the bones of the upper and lower arm is the key here. Improper timing of the two primary movements will cause the punch to graze the target in either an upward or downward direction diminishing the forward motion; and, consequently, diminishing impact force as well. In Figure 7, you are in the ready position with a target in front of you. The arrow depicts your direction of force; the dotted line depicts your line of drive.

In Figure 8, your punch is half extended. Note the rising, forward motion of the upper arm and the lowering, forward motion of the lower arm. With one portion of the arm moving upward and the other moving downward, the weapon (fist) follows the line of drive if both movements are timed properly. In Figure 9, your movement is completed, and all of your motion accomplished propelling the fist in a straight line into the target. These are the basic mechanics of the straight-line punch.

Figure 10

Figure 11

Figure 12

In Figures 10 through 12, we're going to use the same straight-line punch, but add two short steps in the direction of the punch to increase impact power. By moving the mass and the weight of the body into the direction of the punch, impact power is substantially increased.

From Figure 10, start your weight moving forward by taking a short step forward as indicated in Figure 11. Figure 12: Extend your punch as taught in Figures 1 through 9 as you bring the left foot forward realigning your stance. The final step and the extension of the punch should end together.

19

Figure 13

Figure 14

Figure 15

Figures 13 through 15: This time we're going to use the same steps to add impact power, but we are also going to apply an upper body tilt to add both impact power and penetration. In Figures 13 and 14, your moves are the same as for the previous sequence, but look at Figure 15. As the punch is making contact with the target, lean the upper body into the blow as illustrated. With this simple addition, both impact power and penetration are increased.

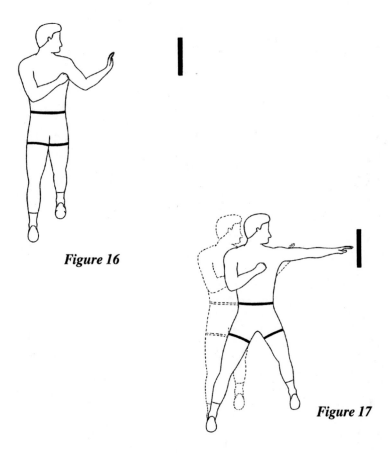

Figure 16

Figure 17

Figures 16 through 22. Over the next seven illustrations, we will be looking at the most powerfully generated straight-line punch. We will be combining the primary power sources of the simple, straight-line punch with a step, an upper body tilt, and a 90° rotation of the stance.

Figure 16: Note the change in starting positions. This is a side-faced view of a right, forward stance. The weight distribution is approximately 60/40, with the dominating percentage being supported by the rear leg.

Figure 17: Take a short, outside, adjusting step with your left foot. Your body weight is now moving in the direction the blow will follow.

Figure 18

Figure 19

Figure 20

Figure 18: Driving hard with your right leg, continue your forward motion and shift your stance to a left forward position. Begin extending your punch as you make the shift.

Figure 19: Continue your shift/rotation movement while continuing to extend your arm as the punch makes contact with the target.

Figure 20: Here your arm has locked through the target as your stance has settled into its new position.

Figure 21

Figure 22

Figure 21: In this illustration, you have continued the forward flow by adding the upper body tilt to the movement

Figure 22: Compare your starting position (dotted figure), to your finishing position in this illustration (solid figure). The distance traveled; the rotation & shift; the muscles implicated in propelling the movement; the lean-in tilt; and, the straight-line extension of the punch combine to wield a tremendous amount of impact power - beyond lower joint integrity if no preconditioning has been practiced.

Part Two: Centrifugal Force Movements

When you change the method by which you generate power, from direct-line to centrifugal force movement, your entire power structure changes. You no longer rely on your anatomical framework being positioned in specific strategic form to transmit positive impact force or to resist negative impact force; target penetration is no longer pre-calculated to access out of range targets or to increase total impact force; and, the multiplicity and complexity of static and motion contraction of skeletal muscles will not be your primary sources of power.

Centrifugally generated impact power relies on the transmission of strength into the rate of motion, (i.e., velocity) of the anatomical weapon, and is independent of both the weapon and the appendage. The potential of centrifugally generated power is virtually unlimited; and like the 90°, straight-line punch demonstrated in Figures 16 through 22, the negative impact force could exceed lower joint integrity. But with centrifugal force powered techniques, the integrity of the weapon itself may be compromised by the mass of colliding forces; that is, the anatomical weapon itself may not be able to withstand the impact without sustaining structural damage.

Observe Figure 23. The center most, dominating structure in the illustration is a pole. A spherical object is hanging from it by a string. All of these objects are at rest in this illustration. Now observe Figure 24. Force is being applied to the pole to rotate it in a clockwise direction as indicated by the arrow at the base of the structure. What happens to the sphere? Because it is attached to the pole by the string, the sphere rotates in a clockwise direction; but it has also moved away from the pole. Why does the sphere not simply move clockwise while otherwise remaining at rest next to the pole?

Now observe Figure 25. The velocity of the pole has been increased from that which was illustrated in Figure 24; consequently, the velocity of the sphere increased symmetrically. In this illustration, the sphere is at its optimum distance from the pole according to the length of the string. Why did the sphere move further away from the pole with the increase of its velocity?

Newton's first law of motion may be defined with the statement that an object will remain in a fixed condition without change, (i.e., either at rest or moving in a straight line as the result of an applied force) until influenced by another

Figure 23

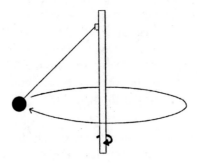

Figure 24

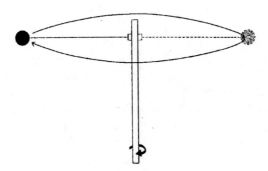

Figure 25

force. Its hypothesis is that an object in motion tends to stay in motion and an object at rest tends to stay at rest. In the study of physics, the clinical term for this phenomena is inertia.

Newton's second law of motion states that objects move as the result of force: a change in speed is the result of acceleration; and, the amount of acceleration depends on the strength of the applied force.

Now look at Figures 23 and 24 again. From the fixed position illustrated in Figure 23, to the rotating position in Figure 24, the only force which was applied was that which caused the pole to rotate. The sphere rotated because of its attachment to the pole by the string; but if we are to regard Newton's first and second laws of motion as valid, we have questions to answer about these two illustrations. If an object moves only as the result of applied force; if an object continues moving in a force-influenced direction until influenced by another force to change its direction, why did the sphere move away from the pole in Figure 24, and even further in Figure 25 as the velocity of the rotation of the pole increased, seeing that no force has been accounted for which either pushed or pulled the sphere away from the pole?

The answer is centrifugal force. Centrifugal force is the force which tends to make a rotating body move away from the center of rotation. As the force to rotate the pole was applied (Figure 24), the effects of centrifugal force caused the sphere to move away from the pole - the center of rotation. When the rate of motion of the pole increased beyond the gravitational pull on the sphere which held it down in Figures 23 and 24, it moved to its furthest possible point from the pole.

Observe Figure 26. This is an overhead view of Figure 25. A third force affecting the movement of the sphere is noted: centripetal force. Newton's first law of motion states that a moving object will move in a straight line until influenced by another force. The sphere is moving away from the center of rotation due to centrifugal force; but not in a straight line. The string, which attaches the sphere to the pole, is exerting centripetal force against the sphere causing it to move in a circle.

With these basic rules of physics understood, picture your body as being the pole; the string as being your arm; your fist as being the sphere; and, directed muscle contraction as being the force applied to the pole. Look at Figure 26:

By generating power into the center of rotation (pole/body), that power is transmitted to the sphere/hand through the string/arm. Neither the weapon (fist), nor the appendage (arm) are being used as a source of power to move the weapon. So, what is the advantage? Why is this centrifugally powered stroke preferable to the multiple power source movements discussed earlier in the text? Lets look at two more illustrations.

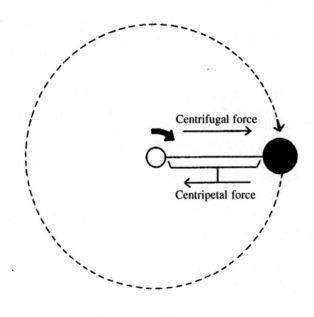

Figure 26

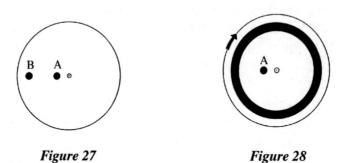

| **Figure 27** | **Figure 28** |

Observe Figure 27. This is an overhead view of a wheel, mounted on a pole in a horizontal position. There are two dots stained onto the wheel. Now observe Figure 28. Again, applying a clockwise force to the pole, observe the visual effects on the dots. At a specific RPM (Revolutions Per Minute), the dot closest to the center of the wheel (A) could be distinguished by the naked eye, but the dot at the furthest point from the center of the wheel (B) would appear to be a solid line on the wheel. It is here that we begin to understand the nature and potential of the power in centrifugal force movement.

Lets say, for example, that the RPM of the wheel is 500. The RPM, if measured at each dot would be the same. Would the distance traveled by each dot be the same? Would the MPH (Miles Per Hour) be the same for both dots? Obviously not. At point B, the wheel is moving at a much greater velocity. This velocity will be realized as impact power when the principle of movement is applied in striking technique.

That principle, coupled with the fact that the mass and the strength of the driving force (the body) is so much greater than the weight and mass of anatomical weapons, dictates the substantially evident fact that centrifugally generated strikes are capable of power far beyond even the multiple power source strikes of direct line movements.

In Figures 29 through 35, the full 360° backhand is illustrated in progressive, overhead views from start to finish. This is a classical centrifugal force movement, and probably the most powerful upper body strike.

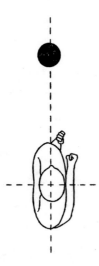

Figure 29

Figure 29: This is your starting position; the round object in front of you is your target. Note that this is not our standard ready position. The spinning backhand may be thrown from a variety of positions; this modified back stance[1] is the most advantageous for my body type and style of free fighting[2]. The leg positions will be studied in the chapter on backhands. Also note the register lines in the illustration. Consider these as being in a fixed position above the figure.

---

[1] Modified Back Stance: even weight distribution, shoulder lined up at 90° to opponent.
[2] Free Fighting: The term used to describe techniques which are not prearranged.

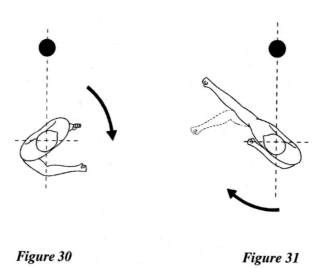

Figure 30   **Figure 31**

Figure 30: The rotation has begun; and the striking weapon has left the chamber position. At this point the acceleration begins and centrifugal force begins to build. Note the position of the head: the opponent (target) is still visible in the periphery of vision. Keep the opponent in view as the rotation begins until the last possible moment.

Figure 31: By continuing to accelerate into the rotation, a substantial amount of centrifugal force will have been built by this point. The arm is now fully extended, and the shoulders have traveled almost half of the distance they will travel to complete the stroke. Note the position of the head. Your opponent is again within the perimeters of your peripheral[1] vision. From Figure 30 to this position, the head is rotated with a snap to minimize the length of time the opponent is out of view. There will come a point in time, after you have practiced this technique and mastered it, that the "out-of-view" time will be insignificant. The spin will be faster than it would be practical to try to focus on the target before the stroke has been completed.

---

[1] Looking straight forward, hold your hands to each side of your head, parallel to your eyes. Move them back slowly till they are out of view. This "side vision" is what is called peripheral vision.

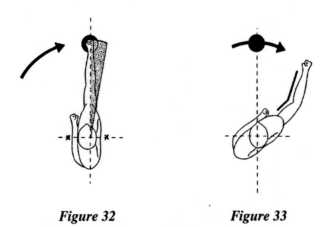

Figure 32   **Figure 33**

Figure 32: Note that upon impact, the register lines indicate the same percentile divisions of the body as shown in Figure 29, the starting position. The point at which the register lines intersect is the axis of the rotation. In order to maintain the optimum centrifugal force, the axial point must remain fixed. If you add or allow another force to impose upon the rotation; the paragon of the natural phenomena of centrifugal force will be compromised, and thus effectiveness in terms of impact force will be lost. If, for example, the head (and consequently the axis) were to be altered to one of the points denoted by an X, or at any point other than as illustrated, the movement would lack its total available power; it could also send the student stumbling across the floor. Without a fixed, solid axis for centripetal force to act upon, the inertia of the movement would pull the student in a straight line away from the point of origin of the drive. Also note the continuum of the drive beyond the target. You do not accelerate to your target, you accelerate into and through it.

Figure 33: Once you have accelerated through your target, discontinue the effort for velocity and go into a "free fall" with your rotation allowing friction and inertial drag to start slowing you down. Note the bend in the striking arm. At this point you will want to exert force into returning the weapon to the chamber position. Also note the position of the head. It is fixed on the target and will remain so for the remainder of the completion of the movement.

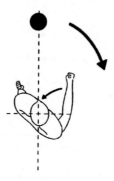

Figure 34

Figure 34: The continued flow from your acceleration will propel you to this point and beyond. Continue pulling the striking arm into your body to return it to the chamber position.

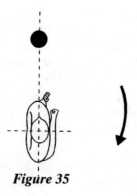

Figure 35

Figure 35: This is the final position – exactly where you started from.

Chapter Two: Primary Movements

Having analyzed the methods of generating impact power for both compound and centrifugal force movements, the next step in our study is to review the five basic strokes which, together with the components of Chapter One, form the basis for the high impact strikes which are the focus of *Neng Da*. Experienced practitioners of martial arts tend to skip studies and analyses of basic forms. Without exception; this habit is a mistake. Basic movements are the foundation for high impact and/or other advanced techniques. Therefore, the more perfect the primary movements are, the greater the capacity for perfecting higher level techniques. Review these movements carefully; your knowledge of them may very well dictate the level of perfection you are able to achieve with the high impact movements.

Straight-line Punch

The straight-line punch is the most basic of all strikes used in martial arts; and though there are a number of variations to the stroke, the primary, direct line principle is common to all of them. Inasmuch as we have analyzed this movement as a needed example for Chapter One, our treatment of the stroke here will be brief.

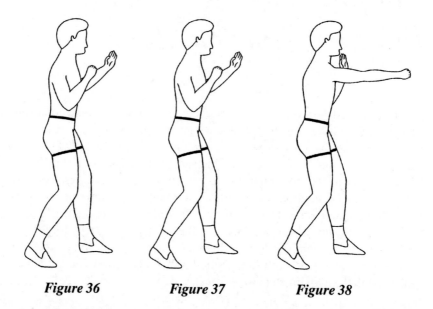

| *Figure 36* | *Figure 37* | *Figure 38* |

Observe Figures 36 through 38. In these three illustrations, we see the chamber, midpoint and fully extended straight-line punch. In this application, the fist makes contact with the target while in a vertical position. In Figures 39 through 41, the fully rotated horizontal position is illustrated. Contact here is made with the fist positioned horizontally. Both the vertical and horizontal positions of the fist are controlled by the allowable movement in the radius and the ulna (forearm bones) as they cross or remain in a parallel position according to the position of the hand and wrist. Though variations do exist between the two punches, the drive principle remains the same for both.

Figure 39

Figure 40

Figure 41

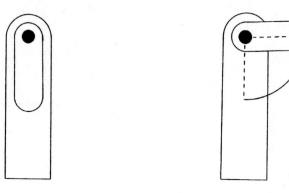

Figure 42   **Figure 43**

There is a carefully timed and coordinated movement required in the upper and lower arm to adhere to the direct line principle which is required to achieve the maximum efficiency[1] of the stroke. Look at Figures 42 and 43. With the punch in the chamber[2] position, the upper arm rests vertically. When the punch is extended, the upper arm is positioned horizontally. From chamber to extension, the upper arm moves upward and forward.

Now observe Figures 44 and 45. Figure 44 profiles a chambered right arm. In Figure 45, the motion of the lower arm is illustrated as moving downward and forward. These two motions, moving with synchronized timing achieve the direct line (straight-line) coordinated movement we seek. Observe this synchronized motion in Figures 46 through 49. The rising motion of the upper arm and the descending motion of the lower arm are illustrated moving in their proper form.

---

[1] Maximum efficiency would require that all movements be directed toward moving the punch toward the target with optimum power, speed and accuracy with no wasted movements or efforts.

[2] *Chamber* or *loaded*, is the term used to denote a starting or resting position of an anatomical weapon.

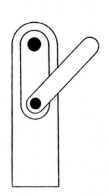

Figure 44

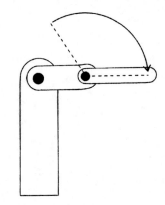

Figure 45

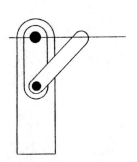

Figure 46

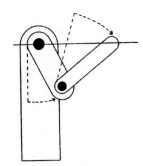

Figure 47

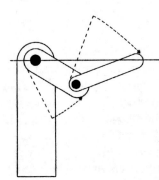

Figure 48

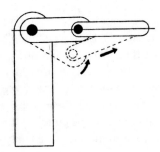

Figure 49

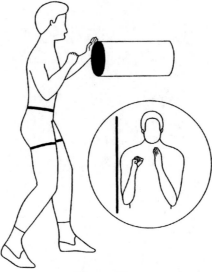

Figure 50

Following the straight line principle also requires keeping the elbow tucked and traveling behind the fist during the extension of the blow. If the previously discussed straight line principle is adhered to, and the elbow remains behind the fist during extension, you should be able to punch into a tube without touching it's sides.

Observe Figures 50 through 52. In Figure 50, note the encircled auxiliary illustration. The punch should be thrown envisioning a wall close to the arm which the elbow should not touch in Figure 51, the punch is entering the tubular structure. The auxiliary illustration at the right shows the path of the elbow from the front view. Note that the elbow has not drifted away from the body. In Figure 52, the punch is extended into the tube. The auxiliary illustration also depicts the punch in the extended position. By following these principles, a straight line punch may reach the point of perfect execution, and will be less likely to be detected by an opponent before impact.

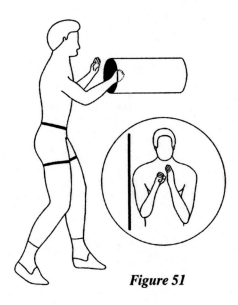

Figure 51

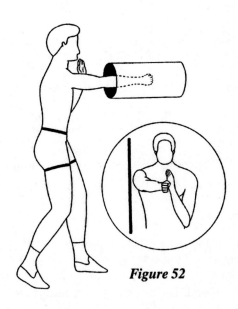

Figure 52

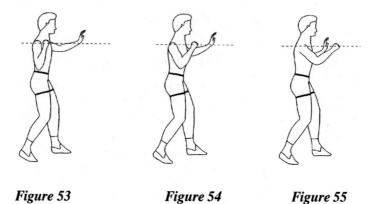

Figure 53   Figure 54   Figure 55

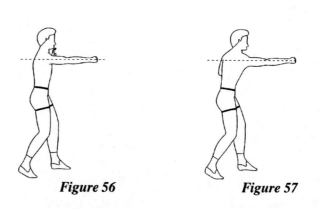

Figure 56   Figure 57

Finally, utilizing a more traditional chamber position, the straight line punch is illustrated again in Figures 53 through 57. With this deeper draw position, the stroke utilizes more of the anterior deltoid muscle and has a greater distance from which to develop speed. However, it is more easily detected, and should therefore not be used as a lead strike.

Cross punch

The straight line principle discussed with sequences 46 through 49 and 50 through 52, applies to the cross punch in the same manner which it applied to the straight line punch. Where the two punches differ is in the direction with which they approach and penetrate a target. All the other mechanisms of the two strikes are the same.

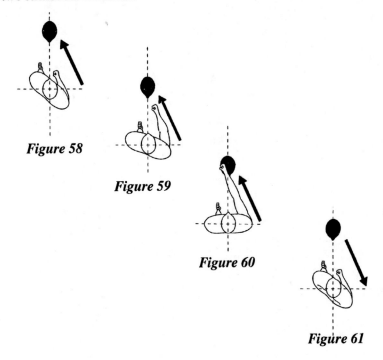

Figure 58

Figure 59

Figure 60

Figure 61

Observe Figures 58 through 61. The target is set at your midline while you are squared[1] to it in a left forward ready position. In Figure 59, the stroke is extended approximately half way. Note the forward rotation of the right shoulder. In Figure 60, the punch is fully extended with the shoulder fully rotated into the stroke. Note the angle of penetration of the target. The punch returns along the same path as that of the extension as depicted in Figure 61.

[1] The term *squared*, or *squared off*, is defined as your being in a chosen position prepared to engage an opponent.

Transition from Cross Punch to Backhand

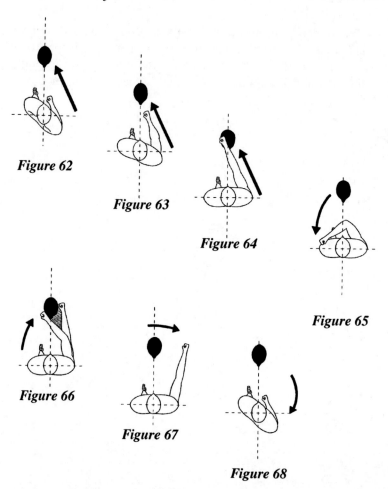

Figure 62

Figure 63

Figure 64

Figure 65

Figure 66

Figure 67

Figure 68

Observe Figures 62 through 68. One very distinct advantage to the cross punch is the ease with which the backhand is integrated into the stroke. Note the transition from Figure 64 to Figure 65. Bringing the extending punch to the position in Figure 65 is accomplished with a continuity and flow of motion rather than a direct separate effort. From Figure 65 to the position in Figure 66, an arc is followed to pass back through to the target on it's opposite side. Figure 67 depicts the follow through of the striking weapon; and Figure 68 illustrates the final, recovered position.

Lead Cross Punch

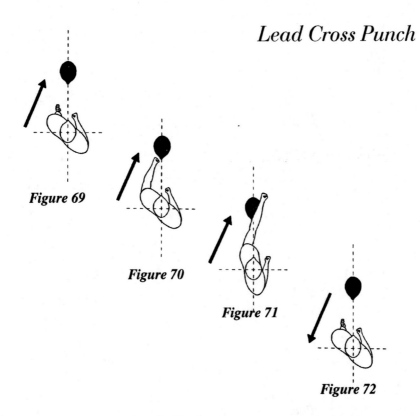

Figure 69

Figure 70

Figure 71

Figure 72

Figures 69 through 72 illustrate the cross punch being used from the lead, (defensive[1]) side. This punch will of course be quicker than the right (offensive[2]) side punch because it will be traveling a lesser distance; but for the same premises will lack the impact force of the offensive side stroke.

Figure 70 depicts the punch extended approximately to the halfway point. In Figure 71, the punch is fully extended and has passed through the target. Note the rotation of the shoulder into the punch to achieve greater penetration and impact force. In Figure 72, the hand and shoulder have been returned to their starting positions.

[1] The side of the body closest to the opponent is designated as the defensive side due to the strategic blocking position of the corresponding leg and arm which rests between the opponent and the student's most vital targets

[2] The side of the body furthest from the opponent is designated as the offensive side which generally follows a defensive side block with a return, offensive blow.

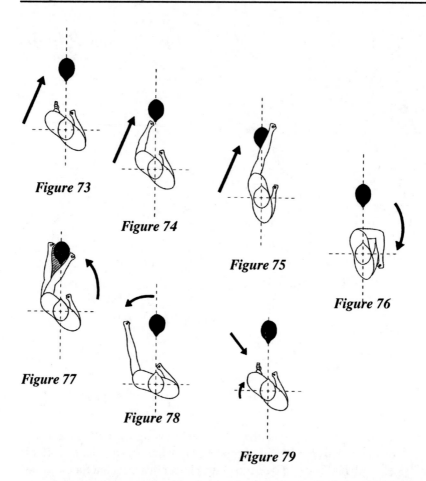

Figure 73

Figure 74

Figure 75

Figure 76

Figure 77

Figure 78

Figure 79

Figures 73 through 79: The follow-through backhand stroke may also be added to the lead hand cross punch. From Figure 75 to 76, this is also a flowing, continuous motion. In powering the backhand, note the positions on the angles of the shoulders in Figures 76 and 77. The shoulder should lead the stroke, i.e., the shoulder starts moving back to the left before the arm begins to open from the chambered position across the body. By powering the stroke in this manner, the greater mass, the upper body, is laying a power base for the extension of the arm which follows on the same course.

In Figure 77, note that the arm is not fully extended before impact, but extends as it passes through the target. This allows the motion contraction of the triceps to add to the total impact force of the stroke. Figures 78 and 79 illustrate the follow through and recovery to the starting position.

Cross Punch: Front View

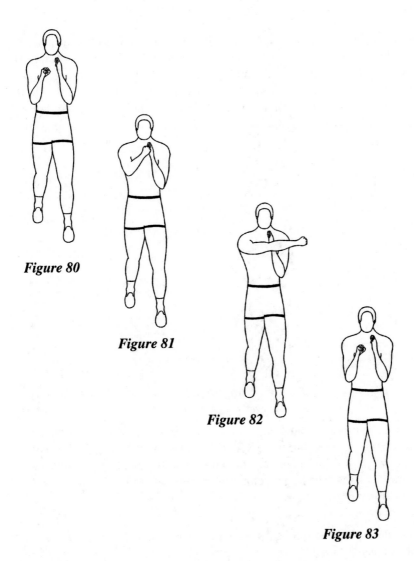

Figure 80

Figure 81

Figure 82

Figure 83

For comparative purposes, the cross punch is illustrated from a head-on view in Figures 80 through 83.

Suto

The suto is one of the more versatile strikes used in the martial arts. Here we will be looking at some of the palm-up, palm-down, crossing and vertical applications of this extremely effective movement as a foundation for the high impact applications to be discussed in a latter chapter. Pay special attention to the rotation of the lower arm in these illustrations as they are keys to the safe, effective delivery of the stroke.

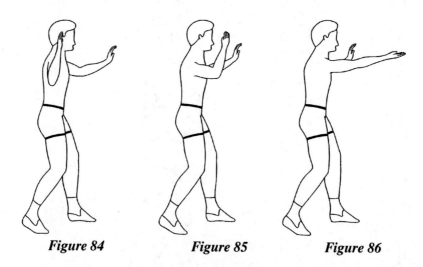

| *Figure 84* | *Figure 85* | *Figure 86* |

Observe Figures 84 through 86. This is your basic, perfect form for the horizontal, palm-up suto. In Figure 84, the right suto is chambered at the ear. In Figure 85, the stroke has traversed approximately one half of the distance it will travel to reach its target. Note the rotation of the hand and the forward advancement of the elbow.

Figure 86 depicts the fully extended stroke; the arm is fully opened[1] and the palm is faced upward. This stroke approaches and penetrates its target on a horizontal plane which will be clearer after observing the illustrations which follow.

---

[1] No upper body stroke fully locks out the elbow. When an arm strike is at it's fully opened position, there is a very slight, almost undetectable bend in the arm to avoid stressing the ligamentation of the elbow joint. Fully locking punches, sutos, backhands or other upper body strikes will damage these ligaments in the long-term.

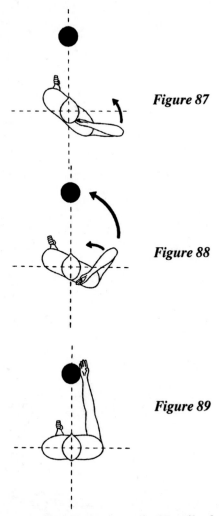

Figure 87

Figure 88

Figure 89

Figures 87 through 89 depict the palm-up horizontal suto strike from an over-head view. Figure 87 is your start position. The right suto is chambered behind the ear and the arrow indicates a sweep motion of the elbow as the initial movement. Also, watch the position of the shoulders relative to the cross lines over the illustration.

In Figure 88, the elbow has advanced about half way to its point of completion, and the hand has left the chamber position. Note that the shoulder has also moved in a counterclockwise rotation. In Figure 89, the suto has made contact with the target. Note the shoulder rotation and the position of the hand.

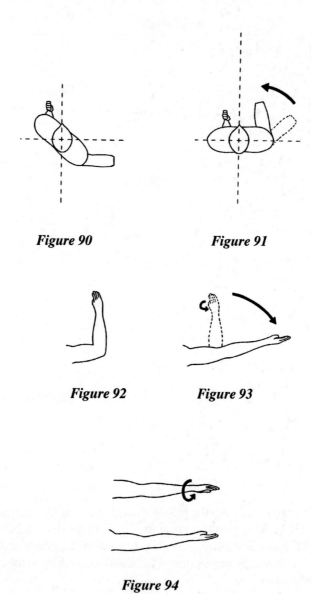

Figure 90   **Figure 91**

Figure 92   **Figure 93**

Figure 94

Look at Figures 90 and 91. These show the path of the upper arm. Figures 92 and 93 show the path of the lower arm and the rotation of the wrist. Also observe Figure 94 regarding wrist rotation.

Crossing Suto

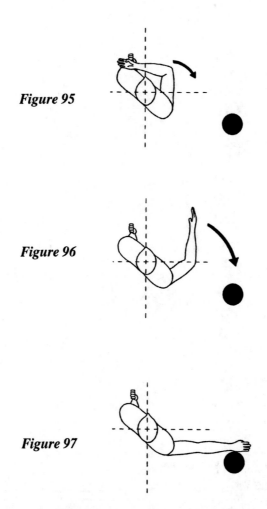

Figure 95

Figure 96

Figure 97

In Figures 95 through 97, the palm-down suto is being applied with a cross body chamber to a target positioned just off the right shoulder. Note the palm-up starting position of the hand.

In Figure 96, the stroke is at the halfway position. Look at the position of the hand. In Figure 97, the suto has made contact with the target and is in the palm-down position.

Crossing Suto without Wrist Rotation

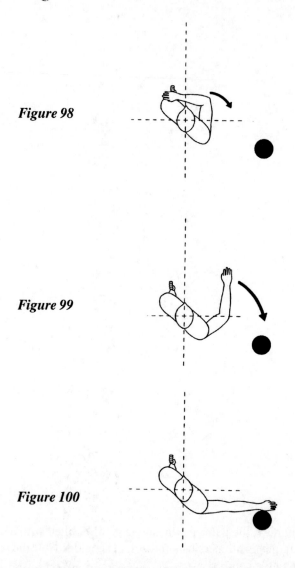

Figure 98

Figure 99

Figure 100

Using the crossing suto without wrist rotation is an option. Observe Figures 98 through 100. The only difference between this stroke and the previous one is the wrist rotation; everything else about the stroke is the same.

Crossing Suto with Partial Wrist Rotation

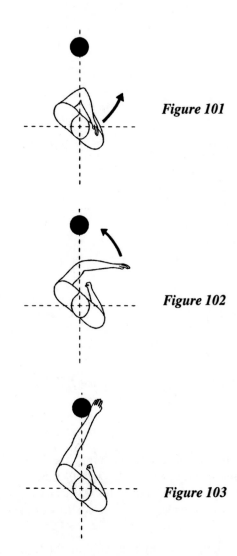

Figure 101

Figure 102

Figure 103

Figures 101 through 103: this crossing suto, applied to a target at the center line, is utilizing a partial rotation of the wrist. Note the position of the hand in Figure 101: the palm is facing the ear. When the strike makes contact with its target in Figure 103, the palm is facing downward.

Vertical Suto

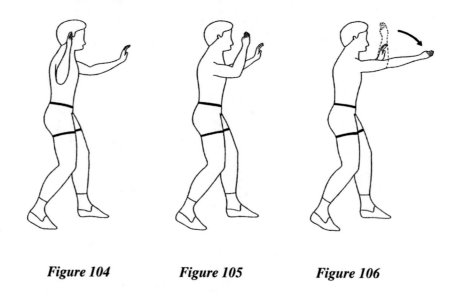

Figure 104   **Figure 105**   **Figure 106**

All of the previous suto strikes approach and pass through their target on a horizontal plane. In Figures 104 through 106, the vertical suto is illustrated. Observe the start position in Figure 104. This is the same position as illustrated in Figure 87, with the exception of the position of the left hand.

In Figure 105, the weapon is at the mid point of its path toward the target. Figure 106 is the completed stroke. Note the downward course of the weapon. This stroke is best suited for striking the clavicle, brachial plexus, sternum, and points on the arms when trapped or blocked and held horizontally. The previously illustrated strokes are best suited for striking the carotid plexus, fossa temporalis, anterior neck region, base of the cranium, and comparably positioned targets.

Backhand

The backhand may be applied as a lead or finishing strike, may be utilized as a speed or power stroke, or may be thrown to any of the vertical or horizontal gates. The student who masters the backhand can move around a rampaging opponent and peck him senseless with long, sharp strokes while avoiding any incoming blows. In its power form, the backhand has deadly, crushing power.

Over the next 21 illustrations, you will readily note the variety of applications in which the backhand is effectively used. Study these carefully and practice them. This is truly one of the most useful weapons in the martial arts.

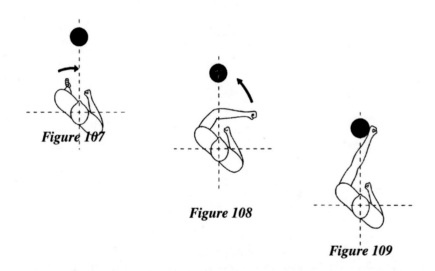

Figure 107

Figure 108

Figure 109

Observe Figures 107 through 109. This is the long form of the forward backhand. The arrow on Figure 107 depicts the direction of your first motion. In Figure 108, the backhand is at its long form draw position.[1] In Figure 109, the blow has landed on the left side of the target. The stroke is applied with a speed snap.

[1] The short form of the backhand would require the fist to ride the center line, slightly to the right, all the way to impact.

Backhand Against Left Side Target

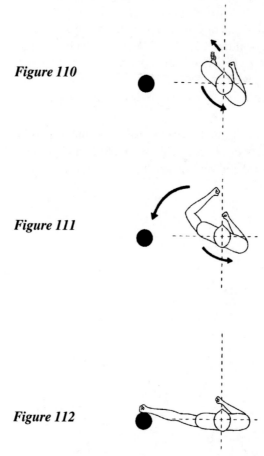

Figure 110

Figure 111

Figure 112

Observe Figures 110 through 112. Using the same hand, we will be seeking a target at the left periphery. In Figure 110, there are two directional arrows indicating a combined, initial movement. Look at Figure 111. The striking arm has moved upward and outward, and the left shoulder has rotated counter-clockwise. Note the directional arrows depicting the continued motion. In Figure 112, the backhand has made contact with its target. In addition to the extended position of the arm, note the change in the position of the shoulder. The shoulder rotation is necessary to deliver the strike without hyperextending the shoulder joint, but it also increases the total impact force of the blow.

Backhand Against Right Angle Target

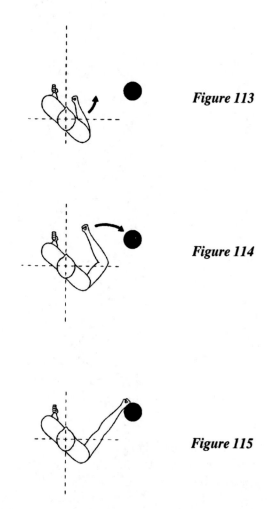

Figure 113

Figure 114

Figure 115

In Figures 113 through 115, we are using the backhand on the right side. Look at the arrow in Figure 113, then look at the position of the elbow in Figure 114. The fact that the elbow leads the backhand is most evident in this illustration. In the final frame, Figure 115, the backhand has made contact with the target following the directional arrow in Figure 114.

Backhand Against 90° Right Side Target

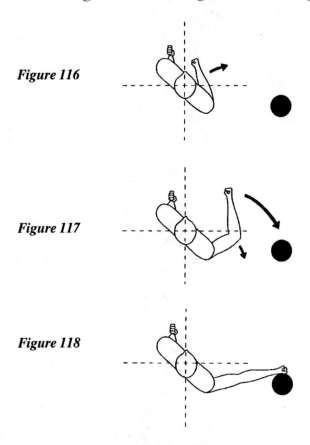

Figure 116

Figure 117

Figure 118

In Figures 116 through 118, we will be throwing the backhand with the same hand, but the target in this sequence is directly off the right shoulder. This backhand will have greater impact force than the backhand in the previous sequence. Why? The greater distance the blow is required to travel to reach the target allows for more speed to be built up, and there is a longer duration of motion muscle contraction applied to the movement.

In Figure 116, the arrow indicates the starting motion of the stroke. In Figure 117, the backhand is at mid point of extension. The directional arrows indicate a combined movement at the elbow and the weapon. Figure 118 shows the completed stroke making contact with the target.

Backhand from Back Stance

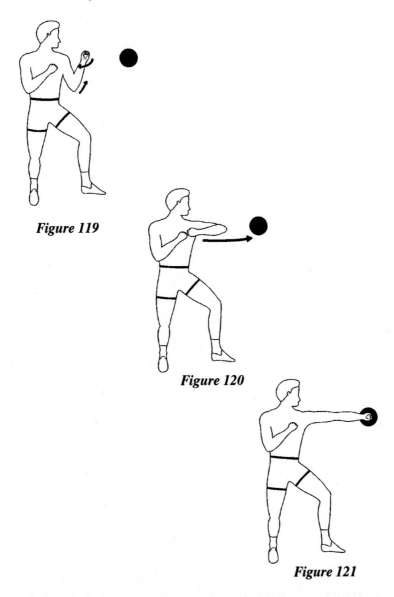

Figure 119

Figure 120

Figure 121

Look back at Figures 107 through 109, then look at Figures 119 through 121. The deep draw position here is used with the back stance illustrated, and is often accompanied by a forward shuffle to gain distance.

Backhand Into the South Gate

Figure 122

Figure 123

Figure 124

Figures 122 through 124, utilizing the backhand into the south gate demonstrates the versatile effectiveness of the backhand. In Figure 122, the directional arrows dictate a movement of the head as well as a chambering of the backhand. In Figure 123, the eyes have been focused on the target and the rear backhand chambered. Note that no other adjustments are indicated in the position of the body. Figure 124 is the completed position.

Inclining Backhand

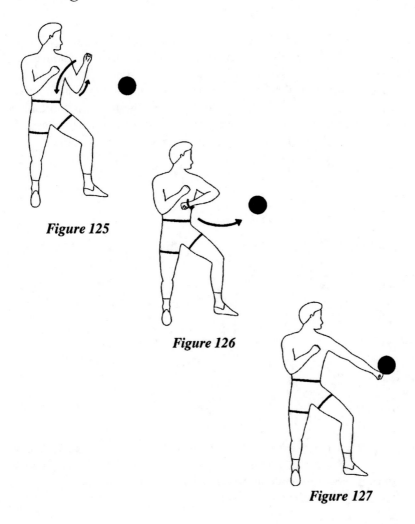

Figure 125

Figure 126

Figure 127

Figures 125 through 127 are the final sequence. Look at the directional arrows in Figure 125 and compare them to the position of the arm in Figure 126. The striking hand rotates toward the body and downward while the elbow rotates upward. In Figure 126, the long arrow shows a rising, sweeping motion while the small arrow indicates an outward rotation of the wrist. In Figure 127, contact is made in an inclining direction.

Palm Strike

Among the advantages of the palm strike are the ability of the weapon to be utilized against solid targets with a minimum risk of damage to the weapon and the ease with which the completed strike may be changed to a grapple or raking attack. As the following series of illustrations will depict, the palm strike may be utilized in a number of directions and with a variety of power sources. Study these variations carefully as three of them form the basis for the high impact palm strikes which will be discussed in Chapter Five.

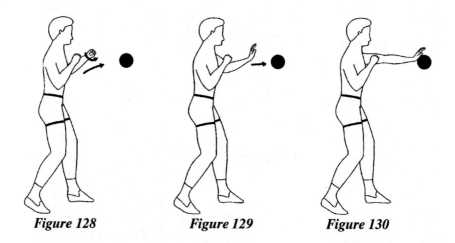

Figure 128   **Figure 129**   **Figure 130**

Observe Figures 128 through 130. This is a short, low, straight line palm strike. For an opponent advancing toward you in a crouch the blow would be directed at the nose. For an opponent in an upright position, the blow would be directed at the sternum, heart or solar plexus.

The arrows in Figure 128 indicate a slightly upward and forward motion of the arm and a downward rotation of the wrist. In Figure 129, note the completed rotation of the wrist and the positioning of the hand for the palm strike. The arm has begun its advance toward the target. The completed stroke is illustrated in Figure 130. The essential elements of motion follow the straight line principles discussed earlier in the chapter as part of the straight line punch and cross punch. Also consider the lesson of Chapter One, Part 1.

Figure 131

Figure 132

Figure 133

Figures 131 through 133 illustrate the same movement depicted in the previous sequence, but this time with the right hand. Again, this stroke would apply to a low target.

Horizontal Palm Strike

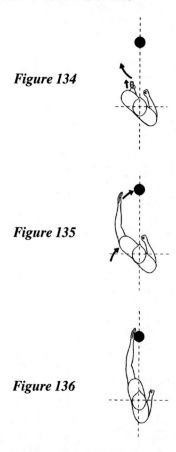

Figure 134

Figure 135

Figure 136

Now observe Figures 134 through 136. Here we see a completely different power source, a completely different approach to the target, and a horizontal position of the hand rather than the vertical position used in the previous sequences.

In Figure 134, the long arrow indicates an outward, sweeping motion of the hand; the short arrow indicates an angled, forward motion of the arm. In Figure 135, you will note an arrow directing the shoulder to rotate in a clockwise motion while the weapon moves into the target. Figure 136 is the completed stroke. Take special note that, upon impact, the arm is not fully locked open. If the arm is completely extended at the moment of impact, damage to the ligaments of the elbow could occur.

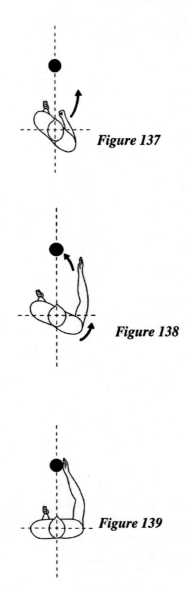

Figure 137

Figure 138

Figure 139

Figures 137 through 139: This is the same stroke as that of the previous sequence, but from the opposite side of the body. Note the rotation of the shoulder; the curved approach; and, the bent position of the arm upon impact.

Inverted Palm Strike

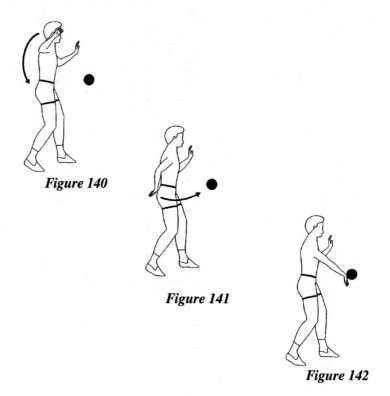

Figure 140

Figure 141

Figure 142

In Figures 140 through 142 we see a completely different line of drive and power source. A circular, centrifugal force movement powers the stroke, and the weapon makes contact with the target with the hand inverted - fingers pointed to the floor.

In Figure 140, note the arrow indicating the initial line of drive. The hand will travel in a wide arc behind the body and the wrist will rotate to the position shown in Figure 141. The arrow in Figure 141 shows the path of the final approach to the point of impact. In Figure 142, the inverted, rising palm strike is completed. The movement from Figure 140 through Figure 142 is a continuous motion.

Horizontal Palm Strike

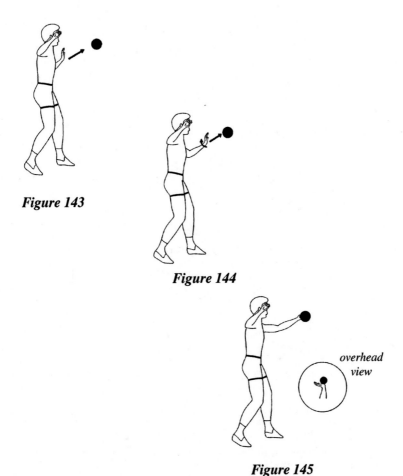

Figure 143

Figure 144

overhead
view

Figure 145

Figures 143 through 145: in this final sequence, the straight line principle will again be applied, but with the hand positioned horizontally.

The arrow in Figure 143 shows the line of drive for the stroke. In Figure 144, the continued line of drive is denoted by the long arrow, and the short, curved arrow depicts the hand to rotate counterclockwise. In Figure 145, the extended stroke is illustrated, and the accompanying, overhead view shows the impact position of the hand.

Chapter Three:
High Impact Punches

Over the next eight sequences we will be studying closed fist, high impact hand strikes, or *punches*. A cursory examination of the illustrations in this chapter will reveal that:

1) The starting positions vary. In two of the techniques we will be starting from a low, deep-set back stance; in one we will begin from a side-faced, forward stance; two of the techniques begin from straddle stances; and, three start from our standard ready position with a slight hand adjustment to facilitate the punches being used. Each new starting position will be analyzed for posture, weight distribution and design.

2) Every technique in this chapter utilizes hip and shoulder rotation from which to draw power.

3) Every technique in this chapter requires one or more major shifts in body weight. These characteristics apply the lessons and logic of *Chapter One* to the foundation movements of *Chapter Two*. The result is optimum impact force.

Advancing Slide Reverse Punch

Figure 146 depicts your starting position: a deep-set back stance. In Figure 147, the standard height for a back stance is shadowed behind an image of the deep-set back stance. The stance we are using in Figure 146 is set low to the ground to allow for an increase in the bend of the legs. This bend facilitates greater use of muscle contraction by lengthening the movement when the stance is shifted in the following frames. The added muscle contraction increases the power of the movement.

The proper posture for the back stance is to position the front heel at a 90° angle to the rear heel; 60% of the body weight is supported by the rear leg, the remaining 40% rests on the front leg. The forward shoulder is pointed toward your opponent over which you are looking. Hand positions are optional and are generally dictated by the intended movements and the   comfort and preference of the individual. The back stance is designed for short, powerful movements and solid, powerful blocking and punching.

Observe the arrows in Figure 146. To reach the position in Figure 148, you will raise the lead foot slightly, step forward and forcefully drive your body forward with the rear leg. The forward hand will be extended as a measuring tool or to grapple the opponent's shoulder/collar area. The lunge forward should be executed with maximum force initiated by the rear leg. The length of the forward leg will set your proximity to the target.

In Figure 148, you are now positioned in a forward stance, the left arm is extended and the right arm is in the high chamber position. Note the length of the advance toward the target as depicted by the dotted figure showing your previous position. To reach the next position, the arrows dictate a rotation of the left hip, a forward motion of the right arm and shoulder, and a return of the left hand. These completed movements are shown in Figure 149.

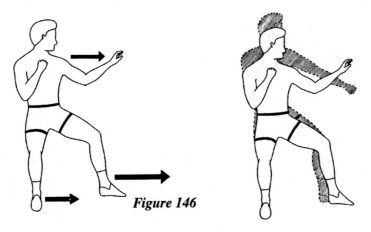

Figure 146

Figure 147

Figure 148

Figure 149

Figure 152

Figure 151

Figure 150

Figures 150 and 151 illustrate the continued flow of the arms till the point of extension of the punching arm. In Figure 152, the final forward motion of the shoulder is illustrated adding the final element of power and penetration.

From start to finish, you have utilized a lunge of the body weight, a stance shift, a hip and shoulder rotation and a primary movement on the straight-line punch: all to power a single strike. These movements are not to be executed as a series of single, independent movements, but as a continuous, high speed flow from start to finish.

Set-up and 90° Rotating Punch

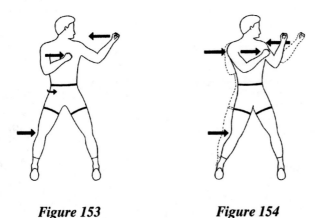

Figure 153   **Figure 154**

In this sequence we will be using a short cross punch and 90°, rotating, straight-line punch. The straddle stance, depicted as our starting position in Figure 153, requires an even distribution of the body weight over both feet. The posture resembles the position of a horse rider: the back is straight, both knees are bent and the feet are pointed forward. In this application, we are facing the opponent over the left shoulder. The straddle stance is designed for short, powerful, movements and power blocking.

Observe Figures 153 and 154. The arrows in Figure 153 show at which parts of the body the starting movements will occur. In Figure 154, the changes in the position of the body are illustrated, accented by the shadow figure showing your previous position. The arrows in Figure 153 direct movements at the right knee and hip and at both hands. In Figure 154, the right knee has been bent toward the left knee; the right hip has rotated toward the left side of the body; the right hand has progressed into a short, straight-line punch on a vertical plane; and, the left hand has begun a return to the half chamber position. The arrows in Figure 154 direct a continued movement at the right knee and both hands with an added movement at the right shoulder.

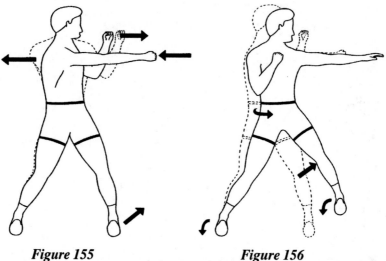

Figure 155   **Figure 156**

Observe Figure 155. This is a fully extended, short, straight-line cross punch. Note that the extension is achieved without moving the feet. We have bent the right knee, slightly rotated the hips and drastically rotated the shoulders to accomplish our point of extension. The left hand comes back to the half chamber position upon impact of the punch.

Now observe the directional arrows in Figure 155, and compare them to the position in Figure 156. The left foot has moved back and toward the position of the opponent, thus the entire body has moved accordingly. The right shoulder has moved backward as the right punch has chambered, and the left hand has extended toward the target as a measure or optional grapple.

Observe the arrows in Figure 156 and note that all of your forthcoming movements will occur below the waist: both feet will rotate counter-clockwise; the right hip and left knee will move toward the target.

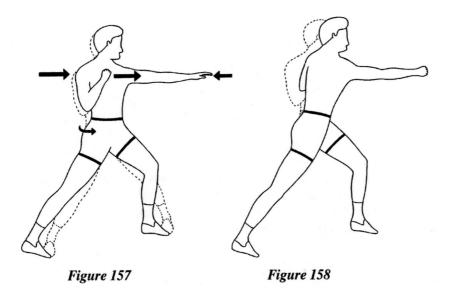

Figure 157   **Figure 158**

In Figure 157, the stance has been shifted to a left forward stance, but we have not yet fully locked the hips forward. Following the directional arrows, our final set of movements will occur at the right hip as it rotates to the left; the right shoulder will rotate to the left as the corresponding punch extends; and, the left hand will move to the full chamber position at the hip.

In Figure 158, the final position is illustrated. Note the difference in stances and body positions between this illustration and Figure 153.

The first punch in this technique is designed for speed, and in this application is used as a set-up punch. The second strike, a 90° rotating; straight-line punch, is our power stroke. The movements from the position in Figure 155, through the position in Figure 158, are one, quick, flowing motion ... not a series of separate movements. Flowing transitions are a key element in power punching. If the shifts in stances and body weight are choppy, power is reduced. Move smoothly, quickly and with deliberate power through all of these movements.

Dropping Lunge Punch

Figure 159

Starting from a deep-set back stance, which we have already studied in the advancing slide reverse punch, we are going to initiate a powerful, forward drive by forcefully extending the right leg while stepping forward with the left, (Figure 159). The left hand extends downward to grapple the opponent's belt.

Figure 160

Observe Figure 160. We have taken a full grip on the opponent's belt and have a right punch chambered for execution. Our next movements are to drop the right knee to the ground and advance the left lower portion of the leg to a vertical position. As directed by the long arrow, the mass of the body will drop downward and forward into the next position.

Figure 161

In Figure 161, our right punch is in the high chamber position and we have a full grip on the opponent's belt. The directional arrows indicate a returning motion of the grappling hand, (left), and an extending motion of the punching hand, (right).

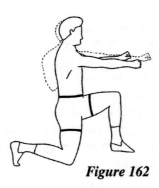

Figure 162

Figure 162 is our final position. As the punch is extended, the grip on the belt is maintained and the opponent is pulled into the punch. Again, flow is important. All of the movements depicted in these four frames are a single, transitional phase of the final; completed movement in Figure 162. The dropping lunge punch is especially effective against taller opponents.

Shift Stance 90° Rotating Punch

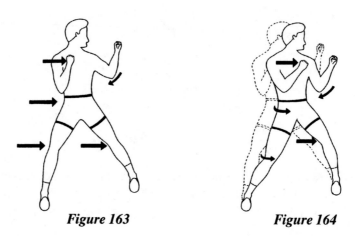

Figure 163   **Figure 164**

The starting position for this movement is a right forward stance. This application is wider than normal to accommodate the stroke we will be using. The normal width of the heels for this stance is just outside the width of the shoulder span. The lower half of the lead leg, in this case the right, is positioned vertically; the rear leg is locked in the extended position. The back is held straight, and the weight distribution is 60/40 favoring the lead leg. The stance is designed to resist the negative impact force* incidental to high impact blows. The ease with which this stance is shifted from right forward to left forward, or left forward to right forward, makes it a practical position to use when planning full powered strokes.

The arrows in Figure 163 indicate movements at both legs, the hips, the punching hand and the defensive hand. In Figure 164, the weight shift is illustrated at mid-point. Note that no steps have been taken despite the distance the body is shown to have traveled according to the shadow figure. The directional arrows in this illustration show a continued flow to the left while the defensive arm progresses to the low chamber position.

* Negative impact force was analyzed and discussed in the book, *Iron Hand of the Dragon's Touch*.

Figure 165

Figure 166

Figure 167

In Figure 165, the rotation of the stance is completed except for the final rotation of the hip and shoulder. Note the arrows depicting the next set of movements: the hips will snap around to a full forward position; the right shoulder will extend into the punch; and, the left arm will go to the full, low chamber position.

In Figure 166, the stance is completely shifted to the left forward position and the punch is extended. The arrow depicts the final movement of the sequence. In Figure 167: The upper body tilt and forward slide of the shoulder is illustrated. From start to finish, all of these movements are a continuous flow allowing the inertia of the moving body weight to be channeled into the single stroke.

Horizontal Shifting Cross Punch, High

Typically, the ready position, commonly used in the series of books published on the Lian shi form will hold the left foot in front of the right foot, and the left hand in front of the right hand. The ready position is the most practical to train from because it is the most natural of the stances. The feet are relatively close together and at shoulder width, and the hands are held close to the body. The stance is designed for both short and long movements, and is easily shifted to power positions as you will see in the frames to follow. The movement we will be studying here is a cross punch used with a shift into a power stance.

Observe Figure 168. The directional arrows indicate that two primary movements must occur to reach the position in our next frame. In Figure 169, the left foot has stepped back and to the left while the entire upper body has rotated in a corresponding direction. The shadow figure in the illustration demonstrates the drastic shift in positions with the single step.

The arrows on Figure 169 direct a number of movements to reach the next position depicted in Figure 170. The left hand crosses the body horizontally to the left; the right hand and shoulder also follow a leftward plane; and, the right foot pivots on its ball rotating 90°.

In Figure 170, the right shoulder is directed to continue moving to the left; the punching hand is directed to advance on a left, inclining plane; and the left hand will rotate at the wrist.

Figure 171 illustrates the completed movement: the high cross punch is fully extended. Note the length of the rotation of the shoulder into the punch and the bent positions of the right knee and ankle to facilitate the upper torso twist. This is a relatively short but very powerful stroke.

Figure 168

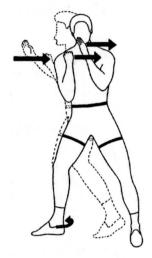

Figure 169

Figure 170

Figure 171

Horizontal Shifting Cross Punch, Low

This movement is basically the same as that of the high shifting cross punch, but here we will be directing our punch on a declining rather than an inclining plane. The opening position is the same.

In Figure 172, we are directed to rotate to the left by the arrows at mid-torso and the left foot. In Figure 173, that rotation is accomplished by a step outward and back with the left foot and a corresponding rotation of the hips and upper body. Both hands are in transitional positions with the right hand at high chamber. The arrows directing our next movements are showing motion at the right shoulder, at both hands and a pivot of the right foot.

In Figure 174, the pivot has been completed and the hip has been rotated to the left to flow with the punch. The inward bend at the right knee allows the hip to rotate easily without binding against itself. The directional arrows indicate that movement will occur at three points to reach the position in the following, final frame.

Look at Figure 175. The directional arrows in Figure 174 show a rotation of the right shoulder which is seen here; a continued extension of the right punching hand which is seen here; and, a continued flow of the left hand which followed the corresponding shoulder, which is also seen in this final frame.

Again, it is important to stress the flowing, smooth transition of these movements from start to finish. It is this continuity and fluidity that allows the various movements to harmoniously generate power.

Figure 172

Figure 173

Figure 174

Figure 175

Full 180° Reverse Punch

Again we will be starting from the modified ready stance, but this time the turn will span a full 180°, and the punch will be a straight-line rather than a cross.

Observe Figure 176. The directional arrows indicate an upper body rotation and a deep back step with the left leg to be used to reach the position in the next illustration.

In Figure 177, our first step is taken. Compare the present position of the left foot with the shadow figure representing its previous position. The step is back and to the outside of the right foot. Note also the increased depth of the bend in the right leg and the leftward rotation of the upper body. The arrows in this illustration direct a continued leftward rotation of the upper body. The arrows in this illustration direct a continued leftward rotation and counter-clockwise pivots on both feet.

In Figure 178, we have, for the most part, reversed our facing direction. As the pivots on the feet are executed, a push off of the right leg powers the rotation. At this point, the left hand is positioned as a measure to the target; the right hand is in the full high chamber position; and, the right hip is poised to thrust into the punch.

Observe Figure 179. The rear, supporting leg is locked and fully rotated, and the hip has progressed into the punch. The right, punching hand is moving forward and the left hand is en route to the low chamber position. Note that the right shoulder is still somewhat back to synchronize with the forward motion of the punching hand. The arrows direct rotation at the right shoulder and hip; a forward motion of the punching hand; and, a continued chambering of the left hand.

In Figure 180, the hip, shoulder and punch are locked into striking posture, and the left hand is fully chambered at the waist. In Figure 181, the shoulder and upper torso add a final thrust of power by continuing to flow with the punch.

The flow of this technique begins with the first step illustrated in Figure 177, and continues till the final extension point in Figure 181. Flow is the key to multiple power source movements. Though the movements are depicted in several stages, remember that they are to be executed in one fluid motion. Fluid movements are of crucial importance to the success and effectiveness of the final power stroke.

Figure 176

Figure 177

Figure 178

Figure 179

Figure 180

Figure 181

270° Rotating Punch with Set-up Punch

In this eighth and final movement, we will be using a short set-up punch with a gap-closing step, followed by a 270° rotating straight-line punch. The straddle stance used in Figure 182, has been analyzed in Figure 153.

Observe Figures 182 and 183. In Figure 182, the arrows direct us to extend the right, lead arm, and take a forward, angular step with the right foot. In figure 183, the right arm has extended into a short, jabbing punch, and the right foot has advanced out slightly forward into a right forward stance. How you follow the arrows and execute the movements to reach the position in the next frame are of crucial importance to the success and effectiveness of the final power stroke.

Look at Figures 183 and 184 together. In 183, the right hand is directed to cross the chest, and the left leg is directed to advance and rotate toward the right leg. The arrow at the hip directs a rotating movement. All of these movements are to be performed simultaneously and forcefully. Whip the right hand across your chest; drive the left leg toward the right; and, whip the hips in a circular motion. All of these movements working together generate power which will be redirected to power the following movements and eventually into the punch.

Having achieved the position in 184, look at the arrows in the illustration, then look at the position in Figure 185. While pivoting on the right foot, step all the way around to the position in Figure 185 while rotating the entire upper torso. Your feet are now planted but still in transition. Note that the arrows direct pivots on both feet and a continued rotation of the upper torso.

In Figure 186, we are in a left forward stance, but still in motion. The arrows direct us to pivot the right foot; rotate the right hip; drive the right, punching hand forward; and, bring the left hand to the chamber position. The flowing, circular transition from Figure 185 to Figure 186 should be assisted by a forceful extension and rotation of the right leg.

In Figure 187, the stance and punch are locked in place, and Figure 188 depicts the continued flow of the shoulder and upper torso to maximize the power and penetration of the stroke.

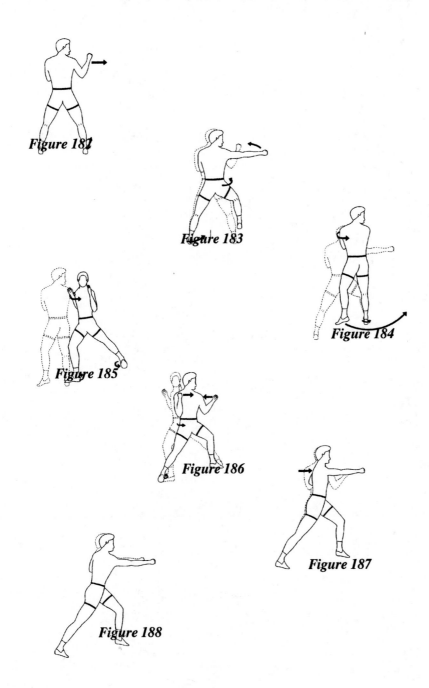

Figure 182

Figure 183

Figure 184

Figure 185

Figure 186

Figure 187

Figure 188

Chapter Four: High Impact Sutos

There are seven high impact suto strikes illustrated in this chapter: four using the traditional, outside edge of the hand,[1] and three using the inside form of the suto. The proper posture of the hand for the inside form is analyzed with the first inside suto technique. Shifts, rotations and stance changes will characterize all of these movements as sources for high impact striking power, and the centrifugal force power source discussed in chapter two will also be applied in this chapter.

Sutos are designed to fit into smaller target areas while providing a striking surface which is both naturally strong and easily developed. The narrow posture of the weapon, and its strength make mastery of this strike a priority effort.

[1] The traditional outside edge form of the suto is analyzed and studied for developmental training in the book, *Iron Hand of the Dragon's Touch.*

Overhand Vertical Suto

Figure 189 depicts your starting position: this is the same, deep-set back stance used in the previous chapter.

Look at Figure 190. You have advanced into a left forward stance bringing the body weight to bear upon the strength of the blow. The right, striking hand is raised above the ear, and the left hand is thrust forward as a measure or to grapple. Note that the hip has not yet been fully rotated.

Now observe Figure 191. Note the distance the right shoulder and arm has traveled. Also note that with this arm and shoulder movement the right hip has progressed forward. The left hand is progressing toward the chamber position.

In Figure 192, the elbow of the striking arm has advanced considerably, and the wrist has rotated to its impact posture. The left hand has advanced further to the low chamber position.

Figure 193: Note that with the opening of the striking arm, the corresponding shoulder has moved substantially toward the target. In Figure 194, the suto is extended to the impact point. Note the lean and rotation of the upper body which has been applied to the final inches of the stroke.

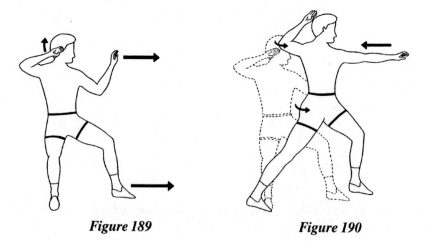

Figure 189   **Figure 190**

Figure 191

Figure 192

Figure 193

Figure 194

Overhand Horizontal Suto

In this sequence, we will be adding a forward lunge and a stance rotation to multiply the final striking power of the basic suto movement. Again, keep in mind that all of these movements are characterized by smoothness and flow. These are not choppy, separate movements, but a series of motions whose effect rely upon continuity.

Observe Figure 195. This is a standard back stance. The arrows direct movement of both hands, a forward step with the right foot and a pivot of the left foot.

In Figure 196, we have advanced to a right forward stance and brought the right hand to the suto chamber position at the ear, (see Figure 189), the left hand is extended as a measure or for grappling purposes. The arrows dictate that movement will occur at both hands to reach the position in the next frame.

Figure 197: Note that the elbow of the chambered hand has moved forward, and the left hand is returning to the body. The directional arrows dictate a continued motion of the hands.

Figure 198: The right, striking hand is substantially forward now; and there are a number of directional arrows to follow into the next frame.

Figure 195

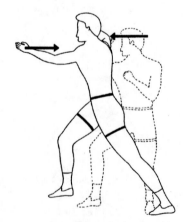

Figure 196

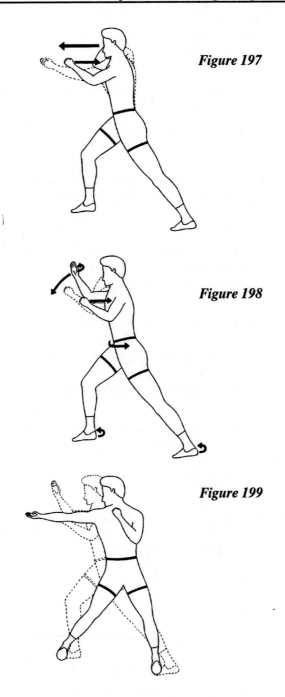

Figure 197

Figure 198

Figure 199

Reverse Palm-Down Suto

Make a cursory examination of Figures 200 through 204 noting in particular the starting and finishing positions. Note also that all of these movements will be going in same direction simplifying the multiplication process of combining the various power sources.

The palm-down suto has a great deal of driving force within itself. When combined with the stance shift and rotation used in this sequence; the final impact power generated by the multiplied power sources is devastating.

Observe Figure 200. Having detected the presence of an opponent at our southeastern gate* we will first turn our head to the right bringing the opponent within the span of our peripheral vision.

Figure 201: Having located the opponent we may now select a response to alleviate any danger he represents. Here we will be using an offensive movement; but there are other options. The directional arrows indicate a step of the right foot and a shift of the left will be used to reach the position in the next illustration. Movements will also occur at the hips and arms.

Observe Figure 202. We are firmly planted in a wide, left forward stance. The remainder of our movements will occur at the hands. The directional arrows indicate a rear movement of the left arm, a forward motion of the right arm and a rise of the right elbow.

In Figures 203 and 204 the continued flow of the arms is illustrated to the full extension and contact point of the suto. Note the low chamber position of the left hand using the traditional form of the blow.

---

* *Gates*, as referred to in this paragraph, denote positions and proximity of opponents in relation to our facing direction. This study was presented in the book, *Danger Zones*.

Figure 200

Figure 201

Figure 202

Figure 203

Figure 204

Spinning Palm-Down Suto

In this movement we will be applying the principle and logic of centrifugal force as a source of power. Our rotation will span 240° or what could also be identified as a three-quarter turn. The impact power of these centrifugal force movements is tremendous and often in excess of the negative impact force an anatomical weapon can withstand without proper preconditioning. You will want to consider the conditioning techniques studied in the book, *Iron Hand of the Dragon's Touch.*

In Figure 205, we are positioned in a left forward back stance. The directional arrows indicate a rising, forward motion of the hips accompanied by a forward step of the right foot and to-the-body movements of both arms.

In Figure 206, we have advanced up and forward to a straight-up position to prepare for our rotation. Figures 207-a and 207-b show where our hands were in Figure 205 (Figure a), and where they are in Figure 206 (Figure b). The arrows in Figure 206 direct a long rotation of the upper body, a rotation of the left foot and a step with the right.

Observe Figure 208. Note the distance of the rotation by comparing the black-line figure to the dotted figure. In our current position our head is turned over the right shoulder bringing the target within the span of our peripheral vision; the suto is chambered at the low vertical position; and, the feet are in a transitional position of the turn. The directional arrows dictate a wide, long step with the right foot, a pivot on the left foot, and a continued flowing turn of the hips.

In Figures 209 and 210, the final resting position of the stance and the extension of the palm-down suto are illustrated. In order not to divert the power of the turn, all of these movements must be a continuous flow from start to finish.

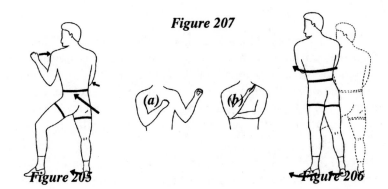

Figure 207

Figure 205

Figure 206

Figure 208

Figure 209

Figure 210

Full Rotating Rising Inside Suto

Before looking at Figures 211 and 212, make a cursory review of Figures 213 through 217. If you are not familiar with the inside suto this movement may create some confusion. The target for this stroke would be the groin, or could also be the anterior neck region or solar plexus if the opponent were bent over at a 90° angle. This blow follows a rising, vertical line and is easily assisted with power by a rise of the stance facilitated by extending the legs.

Now observe Figures 211 and 212. These two views of the inside suto show the exact contact point and the proper posture of the hand. Note that the hand is bent to the outside of the arm and the thumb is pulled across the inside of the hand to keep it out of the way.

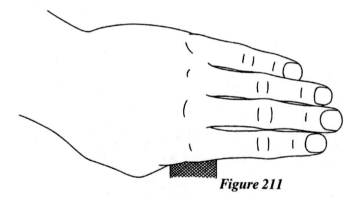

Figure 211

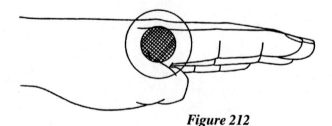

Figure 212

Now observe Figure 213. We are in a deep-set back stance and the directional arrows dictate a variety of movements of the legs and a rise of the right, striking hand. The left foot will move forward and the right foot will pivot counterclockwise as the right knee simultaneously rotates and locks.

In Figure 214, we have advanced into a left forward stance and positioned the right striking hand for a long, centrifugal force rising inside suto. The directional arrow shows the path the blow will follow.

Observe Figure 215. The striking arm is now extended and locked into impact posture. Note the directional arrows. The long arrow shows the continued path of the blow; the arrow at the thorax indicates a rotational movement of the upper body; and, the wide arrow denotes a planned drop of the stance and body weight.

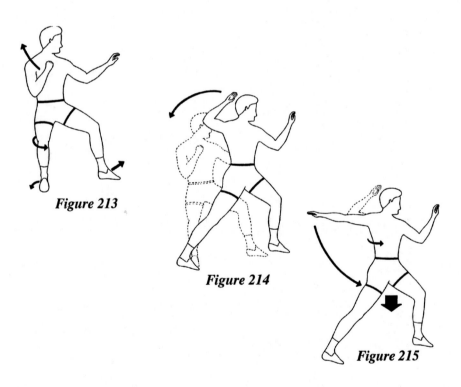

Figure 213

Figure 214

Figure 215

Study Figure 216 closely. Look at the dotted figure illustrating our previous position as opposed to our current position illustrated by the black-lined figure. Note that the hips and shoulders are now aligned to the facing direction and the stance has been lowered as the striking arm reached the vertical position. The body is fully poised at this point for optimum inclining striking power. The directional arrows show the final path of the striking hand; the chambering of the left hand, the planned rise of the stance by justifying the knee positions for the forward stance; and, the forward rotation of the right shoulder.

Your final striking position is illustrated in Figure 217. Note the rise of the stance which adds the motion of moving body weight to the direction of the inclining blow.

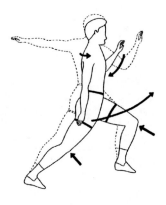

Figure 216

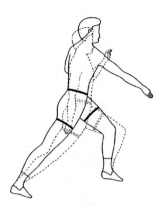

Figure 217

Advancing Inside Suto

In this technique we will again be studying an inside suto using centrifugal force as part of the power source, but this time we will be approaching and making contact with our target on a horizontal plane. Advancing our stance and body rotation will also play a part in adding impact power to the completed stroke.

Observe Figure 218. Here we are starting from our standard ready stance. Our target is positioned at the center of our north gate which will require an outside adjusting step to line the target up with the path of the intended blow. The directional arrows at the feet show that two steps are planned and the arrows at the hands indicate a high chambering of the right striking hand and a blocking motion of the left. Observe Figure 219. Note how far outside and how deep into the position of the target these steps have taken us. The directional arrow indicates an extension of the striking arm.

Figure 218

Figure 219

Now look at Figure 220. The directional arrows show a rotation of the upper body and a return of the left blocking hand.

In Figure 221, the forward stance has been justified to a full forward position with the striking arm still extended backward. The directional arrows indicate a forward motion of the striking hand and corresponding shoulder, and a continued chambering motion of the left hand.

Figure 222 illustrates the final impact position. Note that the upper body is fully thrust forward into the blow.

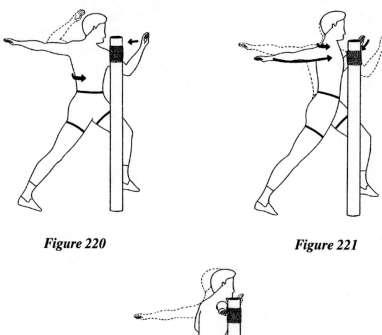

Figure 220   **Figure 221**

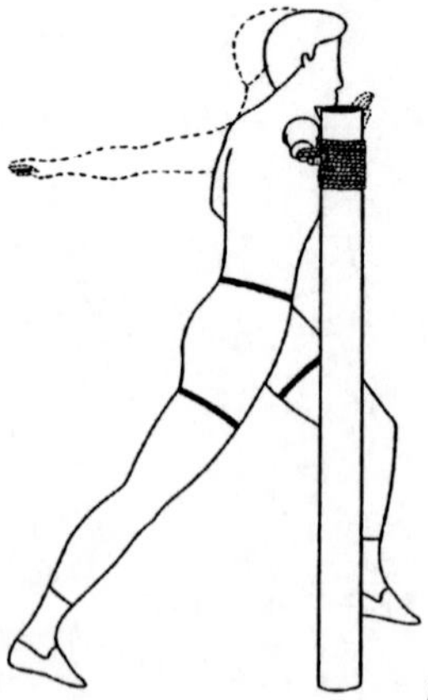

Figure 222

Ninety Degree Rotating Inside Suto

The final movement of this chapter will be primarily the same as the previous strike, but this time we are going to boost the impact power by changing our starting position and adding ninety degrees of body rotation to the movement. When you add positive motion you add to the total impact force.

Observe Figure 223. Here we are starting from a side-faced right forward stance. The target is centered slightly to the front of the right shoulder. The directional arrows show a drop of the right hand, a forward motion of the left hand, and a long, outside step with the left foot.

Figure 224: Note the long reaching posture of this extended transitional position. We are moving toward a standard forward stance from Figure 223, and this illustration is provided as a "how to" view of the reaching step required to put the body within the appropriate proximity to the target to settle into a forward stance and be in range to use the horizontal inside suto.

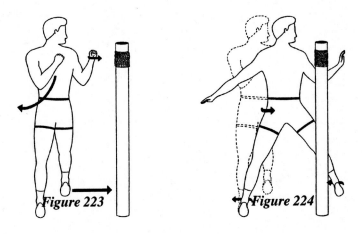

Figure 225: By following the arrows in Figure 224 we will settle into the yet incomplete forward stance illustrated here. Note that the striking hand has

begun to rise. The directional arrows show a continued rise of the striking hand, a rotation of the upper body and a return of the left hand.

Figure 226, the forward stance is now fully justified and the suto has risen to its striking height. The directional arrows show a forward motion of the striking hand and shoulder and a chambering of the left hand.

Figure 227 is the final striking position. Note the lean-in at impact.

Figure 225

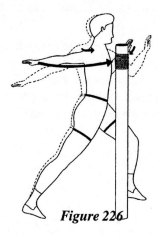
Figure 226

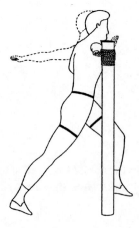
Figure 227

Chapter Five: High Impact Palms

In this chapter we will be studying high impact palm strikes. Unlike the previous chapter, all of the techniques analyzed here will be powered by centrifugal force. In four of the five techniques, we will be using stance rotations and body weight shifts to facilitate this power source.

In the first two illustrations we will be looking at a modified ready stance. It is not necessary to use this modification. You can begin all these techniques from the standard form and make the hand adjustments as you begin the movements, but the modification makes the techniques easier to execute.

The last technique is a three stroke combination utilizing strikes which have been studied earlier in the chapter. This should simplify learning the combination.

Horizontal Rotating Palm

Figure 230. We are starting from our modified ready stance with our target outside of our hand range. The directional arrow shows that we will be taking a forward step to close the gap. The term close the gap or closing the gap, refers to steps, shifts or leans which are used to bring your body within the required range.

Figure 231. Here we have advanced on the target by stepping into a left forward stance. The next phase of the movement is indicated by the directional arrow and will be confined to the left; striking hand.

Figure 232. The left, striking hand is now outside of the target and in striking posture. The directional arrows at the feet and hips indicate a rightward rotation of the stance; and, the arrow at the striking hand directs the final movement to the impact point .

Figure 233. As the striking hand makes contact with the target, the whole of the body weight is driven into the target with the simultaneous shift into the direction of the incoming blow. Be sure to keep the striking arm slightly bent and rigid at impact to avoid hyperextending the elbow joint.

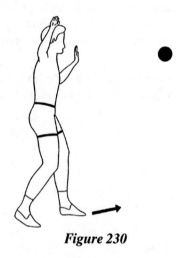

Figure 230

Figure 231

Figure 232

Figure 233

Circular Rising Palm

Figure 234. Again we are starting from the modified ready stance, and will use a gap closing step with the left foot as an initial movement. This will be a much longer stroke applying the centrifugal force principle to generate the primary source of power.

Figure 235. Having advanced our body into the proper range, the striking hand is immediately sent on its way to the target. Note the long arrow directing a backward path of the striking hand. Notice also that the upper body is directed to rotate to the right.

Figure 236. Notice that the upper torso is cocked back to the right, and the striking arm is fully extended back as well. The directional arrows show three forthcoming movements: the striking hand to travel in a long, counterclockwise arc toward the target; the upper torso to rotate toward the target; and, the mass of the body weight to move downward.

Figure 237. At this point, the striking hand is traveling at its maximum possible velocity toward the target with the hand and arm fixed in their striking posture. The stance has been dropped slightly by increasing the bend in the knees, and the upper torso has rotated toward the target. The arrows direct the final movements to be the rising of the stance, which will allow the muscles of the lower body to add impact power to the blow; the forward rotation of the right shoulder; the chambering of the left hand; and, the final movement to impact of the anatomical weapon.

Figure 238. This is the final striking position. Look back through each of the illustrations in this technique and note the distance the striking hand has traveled and the number of movements involved in powering the stroke.

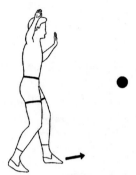

Figure 234

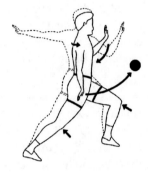

Figure 237

Figure 235

Figure 238

Figure 236

Block & Downward Vertical Palm

Figure 239. This will be a short block and return technique designed to incorporate speed, power and efficiency into the movement. In the Circular Rising Palm, we attacked a low positioned target; here we will be attacking a high positioned target which could be either the right or left side clavicle or the septal cartilage.* The directional arrows show a drop in the right hand and a rise in the left to bring us to our next position.

Figure 240. The right hand is now at midpoint to the position of the palm-down block, and the left striking hand is on the way up to the high chamber position for the downward strike. The arrow at the right foot directs us to step back this time, and the arrows at the hands direct us to continue chambering the palm strike and to complete the block.

Figure 241. We are now in a full, left forward stance as the result of the step taken with the right foot, and the right, low palm block is completed. The arrows direct us to begin returning the blocking hand to the high chamber position and to begin the downward stroke of the striking hand.

Figures 242 and 243. Note the rise of the right hand and the descent of the left in these two illustrations. The right is en route to the high chamber position while the left, striking hand is progressing toward the target.

Figure 244. At impact; the upper body rotates into the strike adding upper half muscle contraction to the blow.

---

* See *Dragon's Touch* for analyses of these targets. Also see *Guge Gongji*, *Da Zhimingde*, and *Gouzao Gongji* for additional technical analysis of anatomical targets.

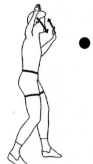

Figure 239

Figure 242

Figure 240

Figure 243

Figure 241

Figure 244

Block & Horizontal Rotating Palm

Figure 245. In this technique we will be applying a great deal of both centrifugal force and body rotation into the total impact force of the blow. There is a mass of power in this stroke, and caution should be taken in being sure the elbow of the striking arm is bent to avoid hyperextending the joint.* The arrows direct us to bring the left hand to the right side of the jaw line and to begin a backward rotation of the right, striking hand.

Figure 246. With the left hand in the proper position; the arrows direct us to sweep across our face for a long, wide suto block. The left hand is still extending backward toward a wide strike chamber position, and the left, lead foot will be taking a backward, transitional step to facilitate the blocking and rotating movements.

Figure 247. At this point, we have made contact with a wide, deep block with the left hand and drawn the striking hand to its furthest point from the target. Having completed the rear step with the left foot, we are now in position to deliver a fully powered horizontal palm strike to a high target. The arrows direct us to progress the right hand toward the target and the left into its arc to the high chamber position.

Figures 248 and 249. With the striking arm slightly bent and held rigid, drive the body forcefully to the left by pivoting on both feet. Draw the left hand to the high chamber position while striking the target with the right.

---

*The book, *Guge Gongji*, which studied attacking joints, analyzed the elbow as a target and taught how to damage the elbow joint by hyperextending it. A review of that section of the book will clarify the need for keeping the elbow bent and held firmly while executing this movement.

Figure 245

Figure 248

Figure 246

Figure 249

Figure 247

111

Three Stroke Palm Combination

Over the next seven illustrations, we will be studying a three stroke palm combination technique utilizing movements studied earlier in the chapter. We will be striking two target areas from three different directions. Our first strike, a downward vertical palm, could be directed at the septal cartilage; our second strike, a left horizontal rotating palm, could be directed at the carotid plexus or the fossa temporalis; and, the third and final stroke could be directed at the groin or at the solar plexus if the opponent were bent forward. You will want to practice this combination for flow and ease of movement before trying for speed and power. The more familiar the body becomes with movements, especially combinations requiring a number of stance shifts, the easier they become to use efficiently.

Figure 250. Starting from the modified ready position, the arrows direct us to begin the downward vertical stroke with the right palm; raising the left hand toward the chamber position for the next strike; and, to take a forward step to close the gap on the target.

Figure 251. Having completed our step into the left forward stance, we are now in range to run our palm strike combination. Both hands have progressed toward their intended positions, and the arrows direct the right hand to make our first strike to the target while chambering the left hand for the second strike.

Figure 252. Here we have impact with the downward vertical palm, and the left hand is drawn high and back for the next stroke. The arrows at the feet and hips direct us to shift and rotate to the right while progressing the left hand to the target and the right to the high chamber position.

Figure 253. Here we have completed the stance shift with the lower half of the body; and the upper half along with the strike itself are following. The arrows direct our hands to the final point of this second phase of the combination.

Figure 254. The strike and upper torso rotation are complete. The arrows direct a number of movements: the feet will pivot bringing the body back to a forward stance aligning the hips with the target; the right hand will traverse approximately half of the distance required to reach the target; and, the left hand will begin its return to the low chamber position.

Figure 255. With the forward stance aligned to the target and dropped slightly to add its rising motion to the total impact force of the blow, we are now ready to deliver the third and final stroke of the combination. The directional arrows show a number of movements: the striking hand to the point of impact; the right shoulder lean into the stroke; the left hand to go to the chamber position; and, to raise the stance slightly by extending the knees.

Figure 256. This is the third and final stroke of the combination. Note that the stance was raised on impact to add power to the blow.

Figure 250

Figure 251

Figure 252

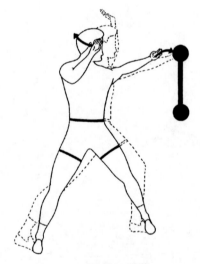

Figure 253

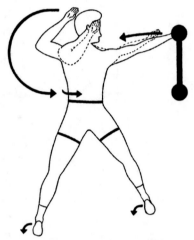

Figure 254

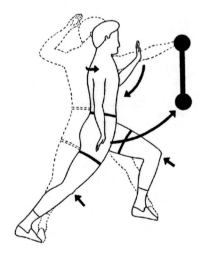

Figure 255

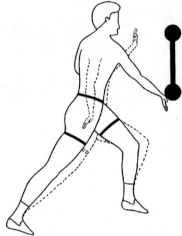

Figure 256

Chapter 6:
High Impact Backhands

In my opinion, the backhand is not only the most useful of the hand weapons, it is the most versatile and the most potentially powerful of all the upper body weapons. It is also the quickest and most difficult to detect. When confronting a lay opponent, the finely tuned backhand could be all the offensive machinery the student needs.

In this chapter we will be studying five applications of the backhand whose design are for high impact striking force. The final technique, is probably the most devastating hand strike practiced in the martial arts: the full 360° spinning backhand. You will notice the characteristic *overkill* use of penetration with these techniques. Because they are centrifugally powered movements, acceleration of the strike can continue through the target maximizing the total impact force and resulting consequences of the effort. You will find these movements to be quite effective.

Advancing Low Block & Backhand

Figure 257. We are starting from a standard ready stance and will be advancing on an opponent who has not yet attempted to deliver an offensive blow. We will be using a low, sweeping palm block and returning a horizontal backhand to a high target. The arrows direct us to step forward with the left foot while positioning the left hand for a low block.

Figure 258. Here we are in a left forward stance which is slightly faced to the inside of the stance. It is at this point which a low gate blow would be defined and our left hand will be used to deflect the strike.

Figure 259. The low, sweeping palm block has moved the incoming blow to the outside of the stance and the long, directional arrow instructs us to raise the blocking hand to the right side of the jaw line chambering a backhand return strike.

Figure 260. The left hand is now in the high chamber position. From this position, the left hand may also be used to initiate a second blocking movement if necessary. The arrow directs the left hand to make a long, circular sweep toward the opponent.

Figure 261. This is our point of impact. The shaded area on the overhead view illustrates the additional range of acceleration which should be applied to the strike. Note the two arrows: the arrow at the right shoulder directs a rotating motion; the arrow at the striking hand directs a continued flow of the movement.

Figure 262. At this point the hand has passed well beyond the acceleration range and may be returned to its starting position. Maximize your speed and power from the impact point of the block through the position in this illustration.

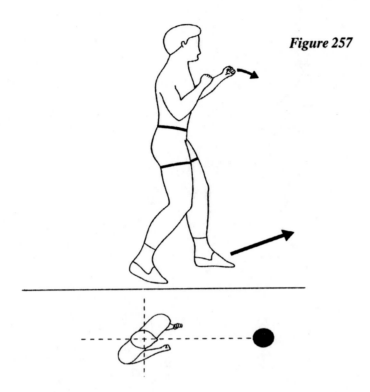

Figure 257

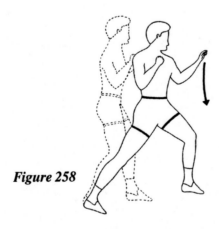

Figure 258

119

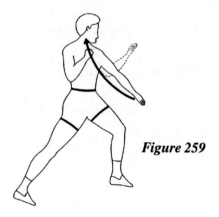

Figure 259

Figure 260

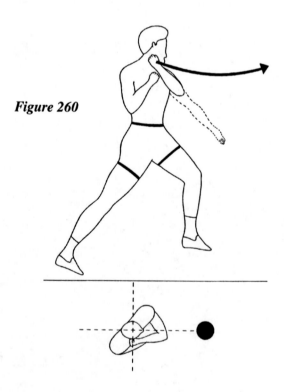

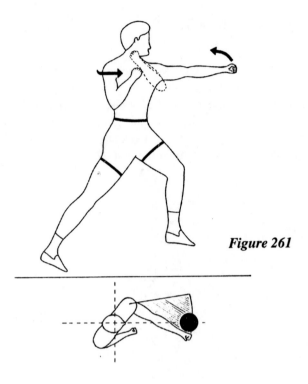

Figure 261

Figure 262

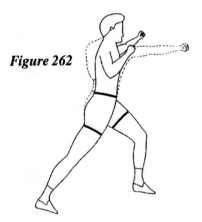

West Gate Rotating Backhand

Figure 263. Looking at the overhead view you will see our target is positioned at our west gate. Striking a target in this position, assuming it was already in range, would only require snapping the backhand out to the left; but as we are studying high power movements, we are going to use our body weight to supply additional striking force to the backhand by taking a backward step. The directional arrows show movement at the left foot and left, striking hand.

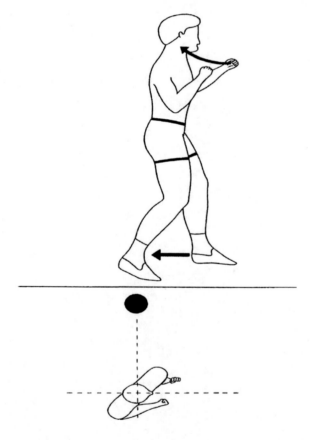

Figure 263

Figure 264. This is a transitional position illustrated to show the passing of the left foot. To take this step you must set the right foot on the floor and allow the right leg to support the mass of the body weight briefly while the left foot is on its way to the next resting position. The arrows direct a continued movement of the left leg and a rising extension of the left, striking hand.

Figure 265. Here the new stance is completed and the backhand is en route to the target. The sole directional arrow shows a continued motion of the backhand strike.

Figure 264

Figure 265

Figure 266. This is our point of impact. We have not shifted stances: the view has been changed from looking off the right shoulder to looking from behind, otherwise the extended blow would be out of sight. If you look at the overhead illustration in Figure 267, you will understand the directional arrow in Figure 266. Again, continue accelerating the blow until it has passed through the target.

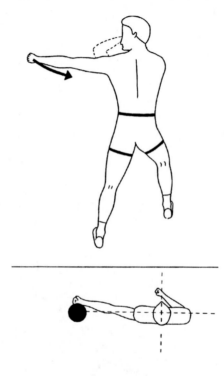

Figure 266

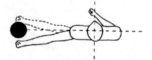

Figure 267

Low South Gate Backhand

This movement is particularly effective against an opponent who is advancing on you from behind while attempting a high grapple. With his hands high and occupied it would be that much more difficult for him to detect and deflect the blow. The first movement we must make upon detecting an opponent behind us is to turn our head to bring him within the span of our peripheral vision. The arrow at the head directs this movement, (Figure 268).

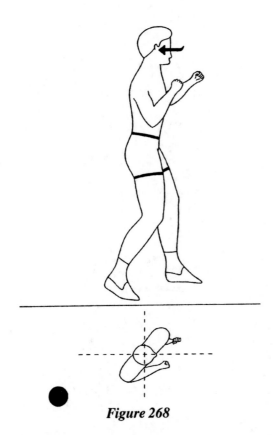

Figure 268

125

Figure 269. Having made visual contact with the target we can determine what defensive or offensive moves should be taken. The arrows direct us to step back with the right foot and bring the right hand to the high chamber position.

Figure 270. We are now in a deep, left forward stance with our right backhand chambered at the jaw line. The arrow directs us to begin a wide, rearward sweep downward.

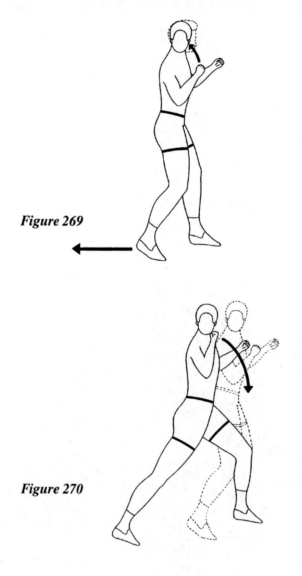

Figure 269

Figure 270

Figures 271 through 273. Over these three illustrations, we can observe the circular arc the backhand travels in to the impact point. For the purpose of clarification, your movements from Figure 269 through 273 are simultaneous. If you separate the changing of stances from the motion of the strike then the step becomes a gap-closing movement rather than a power assisting action. The impact of the strike and the setting of the stance are to be completed simultaneously in order to synchronize the powers of both movements into one striking force.

Figure 271

Figure 272

Figure 273

High South Gate 90° Rotating Backhand

Figure 274. In our previous technique; we attacked a south gate target with a rising, vertical backhand; in this technique we will be attacking a high south gate target with a horizontal approach using a 90° rotation to add power to the stroke. Beginning from a ready position, we will again turn our head to use our peripheral vision to make eye contact with the target while bringing the right backhand to the high chamber position.

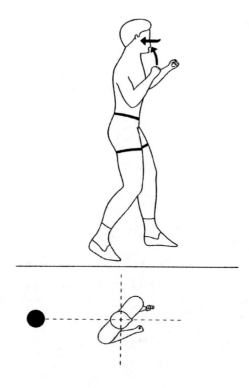

Figure 274

Figure 275. Having made visual contact with the target and chambering our backhand, our next movements will occur at the feet by stepping around with the right foot and pivoting with the left. We will also be rotating the mass of the upper body as we take our step.

Figure 276. Here our body has traveled 90° in the direction of the blow bringing the strength of the motion and the body weight to bear upon the total impact of the strike. The arrows direct us to justify the forward stance by setting the right foot flat on the floor and locking the corresponding knee, and bringing the left hand closer to the center line in the event it would be needed for defensive purposes.

Figure 275

Figure 276

Figure 277. These three graphs, a, b and c, represent the foot positions of Figures 274, 276 and 278, respectively.

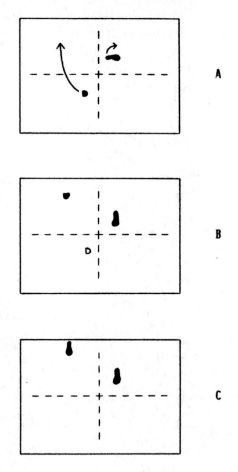

In Figure 278, the stance is locked with the backhand directed to begin its journey to the target.

Figures 279 through 281. These three figures show the extension and trajectory of the finished backhand. All of the movements from the final locking of the forward stance in Figure 278 through the extension of the backhand in Figure 281, are to be completed simultaneously to insure the synchronization of the several movements. This is necessary to optimize the power output of the blow.

Figure 278

Figure 279

Figure 280

Figure 281

Full 360° Spinning Backhand

The full 360° spinning backhand will be the final technique studied in *Neng Da*. We studied this movement briefly in chapter one and that analysis and set of illustrations will be reviewed here again. We will then view the technique from a side view assisted by two corresponding graphs which will appear with each anatomical figure. Study all of these carefully. When you have mastered the 360° backhand, you have truly mastered a devastating weapon.

Figure 282. This is your starting position: the round object in front of you is your target. Note that this is not our standard ready position. The spinning backhand may be thrown from a variety of positions; this modified back stance is the most advantageous for my body type and style of free fighting. The leg positions will be studied with Figures 289 through 295. Also note the register lines in these illustrations. Consider these as being in a fixed position above each figure.

Figure 283. The rotation has begun, and the striking weapon has left the chamber position. At this point the acceleration begins and centrifugal force begins to build. Note the position of the head: the opponent (target) is still visible in the periphery of vision. Keep the opponent in view as the rotation begins until the last possible moment.

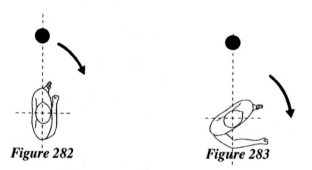

Figure 282   **Figure 283**

Figure 284. By continuing to accelerate into the rotation, a substantial amount of centrifugal force will have been built by this point. The arm is now fully extended and the shoulders have traveled almost half of the distance they will travel to complete the stroke. Note the position of the head. Your opponent is again within the perimeters of your peripheral vision. From Figure 283 to this position, the head is rotated with a snap to minimize the length of time the opponent is out of view. There will come a point in time; after you have practiced this technique and mastered it, that the *out of view* time will be insignificant: the spin will be faster than it would be practical to try to focus on the target before the stroke has been completed.

Figure 285. Note that, upon impact, the register lines indicate the same percentile divisions of the body as shown in Figure 282, the starting position. The point at which the register lines intersect is the axis of the rotation. In order to maintain the optimum centrifugal force; the axial point must remain fixed. If you add or allow another force to impose upon the rotation, the paragon of the natural phenomena of centrifugal force will be compromised, and thus effectiveness in terms of impact force will be lost. If, for example, the head (and consequently the axis) were to be altered to one of the points denoted by an x, or at any point other than as illustrated, the movement would lack its total available power and could send the student stumbling across the floor. Without a fixed, solid axis for centripetal force to act upon, the inertia of the movement would pull the student in a straight line away from the point of origin of the drive. Also note the continuum of the drive beyond the target. You do not accelerate to your target; you accelerate into and through it.

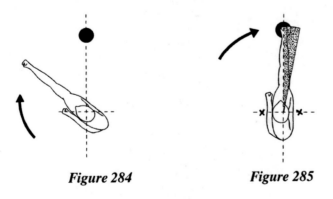

Figure 284   **Figure 285**

Figure 286. Once you have accelerated through your target, discontinue the effort for velocity and go into a *free fall* with your rotation allowing friction and inertial drag to start slowing you down. Note the bend now in the right, striking arm. At this point, you will want to exert force into returning the weapon to the chamber position. Also note the position of the head. It is fixed on the target and will remain so for the remainder of the completion of the movement.

Figure 287. The continued flow from your acceleration will propel you to this point and beyond. Continue pulling the striking arm into your body to return it to the chamber position.

Figure 288. This is the final position—exactly where you started from.

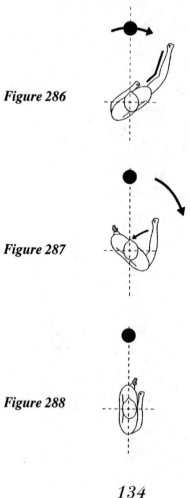

Figure 286

Figure 287

Figure 288

Figure 289. Now we are going to observe a full anatomical figure going through the spinning backhand beginning from a ready position. Consider yourself looking at the illustrations from eye level to the floor. Both feet are on the floor in this figure. The circular graph at the bottom of the illustration shows the position of the feet on the floor; the rectangular graph shows the facing position of the upper body.

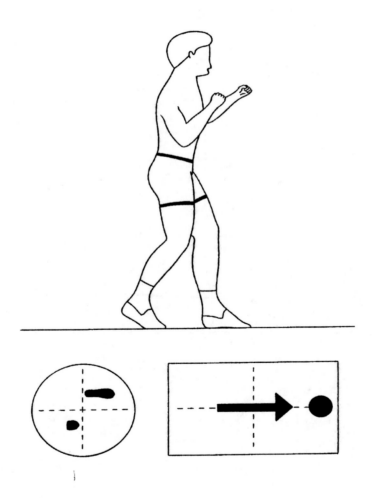

Figure 290. Having begun our rotation; the upper body is turned to the right and the feet have pivoted to that direction.

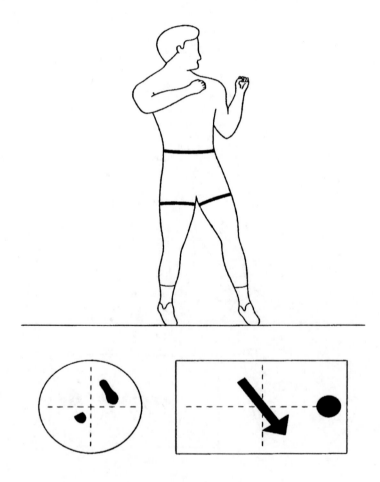

Figure 291. Note that both feet have left the floor completely. The   back-hand is drawn high to the chin.

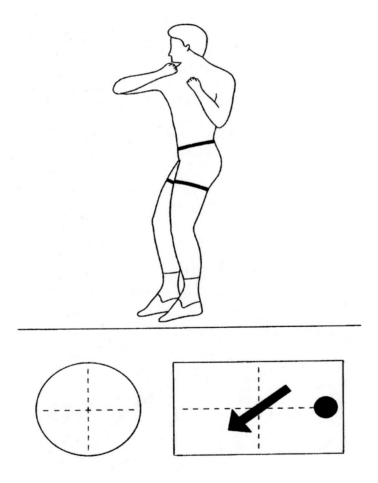

Figure 292. As the rotation continues centrifugal force is being built.

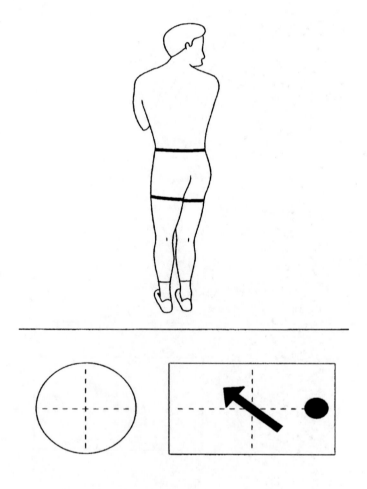

Figure 293. Note the facing direction of the upper body and the extension of the blow. This is your point of impact, but note that the feet are still not in contact with the floor. If the feet were touching the floor they would be putting a drag on the rotation and consequently upon the force of the blow as well.

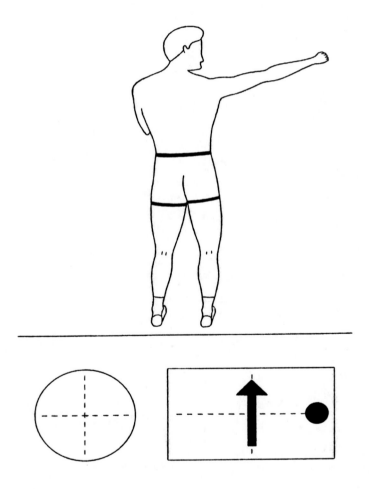

Figure 294. With the blow well through the target, the left foot is now back on the floor as the spin continues toward the starting position.

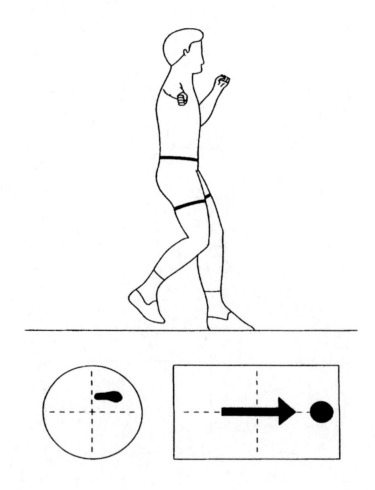

Figure 295. Here we are back to our starting position. For some people this free spin technique comes easily; for others it is nearly impossible. Most students try to leap into the air as they start their spin which causes a problem in splitting the effort of the many muscles involved in the movement. Do not elevate your body any further than is necessary to clear the surface upon which you are standing. Concentrate on your rotation rather than your height.

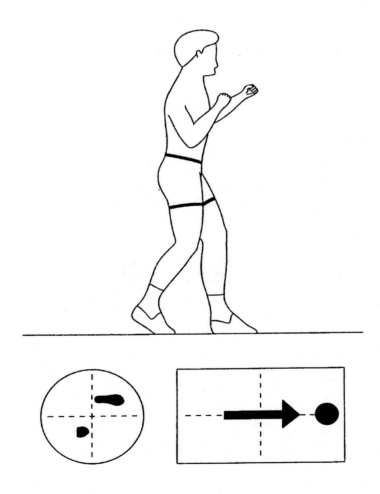

Conclusion

Some years ago, I had occasion to observe an incident in which two men were involved in a physical confrontation against one man. I was seated when it began; I was seated when it ended. I was with an associate at the time whose judgment of the situation was apparently opposite of my own. When it was over, he looked at me and said, "I don't know how you could sit there and watch that." He was aware of my skills and had determined that my having them put me under some obligation to interfere. He and I were both aware of the circumstances which lead to the dispute.

This associate had made three significant, moral judgments. First, he made the judgment that the two men were wrong to engage the single opponent. Second, he made the judgment that my skills subjected me to some unwritten, obligatory standards which demanded my defense of the single opponent; and third, he made the judgment that I had acted improperly by my failure to intervene on behalf of the individual combatant.

Approximately four years before the incident described above, I was involved in a physical confrontation during which I unleashed a fully powered, 180° crescent kick on an opponent which sent him sailing across a theater lobby. His neck and jaw were shattered from the single stroke. He had not raised his hands against me; he had not approached me in an aggressive, hostile manner; he had done nothing to threaten or endanger me in any way.

In a manner of speaking, a skilled martial artist is "the only guy in town with a gun"; he wields the weapon of devastation at will. Just as easily as one with such skills can be an asset to friends, family and the community at large, that same person can become a tyrant, enforcing his own will and brand of justice upon others, be it right or wrong. A Chinese philosopher said a man is three things: what he sees himself to be; what others see him to be; and, what he really is. Which of these are most important to you? When the sword is in your hand, or you are the only person with a gun, the burden of responsibility comes to bear upon your character, your moral, ethical judgments and your actions. Since morality and judgments have no objective bases, it would be wise to endeavor to understand your own   rationale in making decisions which may affect perhaps the very existence; of other people.

A number of questions arise from the challenges of deciding what is a right or a wrong decision, and if we are either right or wrong in acting, (or not) upon our decisions. Philosophers have wrestled with these and related questions for centuries; while different societies adhere to established moral codes which are as far from a basic, universal formula as day is from night. In some parts of the world a child is left to fend for food and his very survival in uncivilized, hostile environments as soon as he or she is able to walk. For a child to be left unattended in a like manner in this country would be considered an appalling criminal act.

The study of these variances have been summarized under four basic terms: ethical relativism which states that moral rules or standards are somehow relative to the attitudes of one's society or group; descriptive relativism, which states that different societies do in fact accept different codes; normative ethical relativism, which states that each person ought to do what is dictated by his society's code; and, meta-ethical relativism, which states that there is no standard of reasoning about morality that is independent of the practices of particular societies.

These hypotheses infer that there is a syntax in the moral fabric of an individual and the community in which he lives. Should the actions and moral precedents of your peers be the yardstick by which you measure morality, by which you decide what is right or wrong? Can we know to be correct, should we accept without scrutinizing, the value judgments the moral parameters of others? Do we not shun our obligation to evaluate for ourselves, the rights and wrongs of moral judgments, when we accept the judgments of others without testing their validity?

Moral principles may be divided into two main types: teleological and deontological. The teleological principle states that the acts which are right, and which we should perform, are those with certain valuable consequences, (also called consequentialism). The deontological principle states that the rightness of an act depends not on the value of it's consequences, but on the nature of the act itself and the intention of the agent. Both leave serious, additional questions.

If we should perform those acts which will have certain valuable consequences, by what criteria do we determine what is valuable? Valuable to whom? Without an absolute or identifiably objective basis, the burden is upon the individual to determine what results are in fact valuable or to rely upon societal standards which may or may not have been arrived at with what we consider to be dignified and proper moral reasoning. And if the consequences alone are to be considered, then by such standards treachery and murder, which resulted in valuable consequences, would also be correct. Conversely, if the consequences of an act are irrelevant, and only the nature and intentions of the act are of any real significance then telling a truth which costs millions of innocent lives is a morally proper act. From this pointy we encounter additional questions.

If we choose to do the "right" thing, why do we do it? Is this a self-serving act, or are we pursuing right for it's own sake or the sake of others? The view that we each seek our own satisfaction in performing a morally correct act is called psychological egoism - that our motive for acting morally is to secure our own happiness. Again questions arise. If we are made happy, if we derive satisfaction from observing good which resulted from our actions, is this indeed a self-serving act, or is it the result of a high standard of personal ethics, the exercise of which brings us happiness because it is ethical?

The questions and discourses on the subject of morality are numerous; and those presented here in brief are intended to stimulate thought; to bring the student to the realization that with harnessing destructive power comes the responsibility to use it wisely, morally, and with discretion. The philosopher whom I've found to possess the greatest, most applicable reasoning to the subject of proper ethics lived in Ellis, Greece, during the pre-Christian era; his name was Pyrrho. The foundation for the Pyrrhonian school of thought may be summed up in six words: "all terms of judgment are relative." What one man regards as a great distance to run may be regarded as a short distance to another. Weight which feels light to one man may feel heavy to another. If in either case we proclaim as to the distance or the weight, and determine that one or the other man's judgment is erroneous, we do not add facts to the questions At hand, but add yet another relative conclusion for one may come after us with an opposing opinion.

It is my opinion, and therefore my teaching, that all terms of judgment are relative, and that there are degrees and severity of right and wrong which will be dictated by the corresponding circumstances. In the case of the two men fighting against the one, the one had repeatedly provoked the two thinking his size and reputation secured him from danger. In my judgment, I would have been wrong to interfere. In the case of the man I hit with the crescent kick, he had forcefully, sexually assaulted one of my young, female students whom I loved very dearly. In my opinion, my moral judgment, my actions were justified. I have never to this day felt any remorse for that action, nor will I ever. That decision was contrary to the moral codes of our society and in opposition to the view of normative ethical relativism, but the decision was mine, based largely on the atrocity of the act against that child.

In maximizing your strength and capabilities in the martial arts, you are creating an awesome power. Unbridled power is dangerous. The decision to use it must be based upon sound, moral reasoning and practical principles. "Right" is not always clear cut, nor is it as simple as justifying an act with subjective or fabricated logic. Neither is "right" always what happens to have been written by other men. If there were a universally applicable formula, which by it's nature and logic, guaranteed justice and an unshakable integrity, I would share it with you. I have not found one beyond the Pyrrhonian principle of relativity which in it's essence demands the consideration of the minutest of details.

Of a surety, you must live with your own decisions. Indubitable truths are seldom found in this world, so we must rely on our individual moral codes to establish our ethical precepts. May yours be of those truths which are knowable, and may you have the courage to pursue them.

Glossary

ACCELERATION: the increasing of speed; powering toward.

ALIGNED: brought into proper relation to; properly positioned.

ANATOMICAL FRAMEWORK: the skeletal (bone) structure of the body.

ANATOMICAL WEAPONS: weapons of the body, such as the suto, the fist, palm strike, etc.

ANTERIOR DELTOID MUSCLE: portion of the deltoid muscle, also referred to as the shoulder cap, positioned at the front of the body next to the muscle of the chest (pectoralis).

ANTERIOR NECK REGION: front area of the neck between the chin and the collar bone.

AXIAL POINT: center of rotation.

BASE OF THE CRANIUM: area where the back of the neck meets the back of the skull.

BICEPS: muscle on the front side of the upper arm from the shoulder to the elbow.

BRACHIAL PLEXUS: net of cervical nerves which form a plexus at the trapezius muscle at the rear upper area of the shoulder.

CAROTID PLEXUS: Jugular Vein and Carotid Artery, located at each side of the neck which provides blood flow to and from the brain.

CENTRIFUGAL FORCE POWER SOURCES: power sources which rely on the principle of centrifugal force through circular body movements.

CENTRIPETAL FORCE: the opposing action which exerts force toward the center of a rotating body.

CHAMBER (POSITION): position of a punch or other strike at its starting point next to the body.

CLAVICLE: collar bone.

COMPLEXITY: the state of involving numerous factors.

COMPOUND POWER SOURCES: involving a number of sources to power a strike or other movement.

CONTINUITY: the state of being continuous or flowing.

COUNTERCLOCKWISE: opposite the direction a clock rotates in.

DIMINISHING: reducing; losing power or force.

DIRECT LINE PRINCIPLE: the concept that following a straight line toward a target from a chamber position increases the power and efficiency of a strike while reducing the delivery time and visibility of the incoming stroke.

FACILITATE: to make easy or less difficult.

FIXED CONDITION: unmoving; unchanged.

FLUIDITY: continuous ease of movement; without strain.

FORCE LINES: (see direct line principle).

FOSSA TEMPORALIS: bony structure around the temple.

GAP CLOSING STEP: a step taken in the execution of a technique which brings the opponent in range of a chosen strike.

GRAPPLE: to take a grip upon an opponent.

GRAVITATIONAL PULL: the downward natural pull of gravity.

HORIZONTAL: parallel to the ground or floor.

HYPEREXTENDING: extending beyond the normal limitations of a joint stretching or damaging the ligaments.

IMPACT FORCE: power resulting from a striking effort.

INCLINING: rising at an angle.

INERTIA: continuity of movement or lack of movement, depending on the state of the object.

INTEGRITY OF A WEAPON, (ANATOMICAL): the strength of the weapon in terms of its ability to resist negative impact force. (see definition of negative impact force).

INTENT: in terms of Martial Arts, it is the concept of being in the decided state of mind to fight with the intent to inflict damage on an opponent or not to fight at all.

INTERSECT: to join or cross, as in two lines

INVERTED: reversed; turned upside down.

JOINT INTEGRITY: strength of a joint.

LATISSIMUS DORSI: muscles beneath the arms along the ribs in the back.

LIGAMENTS: the connective tissues which bind the bones of the skeleton to each other forming joints.

LINE OF DRIVE: the prescribed path a strike is to follow to yield maximum efficiency from the effort; see also DIRECT LINE PRINCIPLE.

MOTION MUSCLE CONTRACTION: the flexing of a muscle to cause movement, such as the flexing of the biceps to fold the arm.

MULTIPLICITY AND COMPLEXITY [of static and motion contraction of skeletal muscles]: the studied and practiced method of muscle movements to execute a perfected technique.

NEGATIVE IMPACT FORCE: the opposite reaction to a striking effort which is felt in and affects the hand or other weapon of the body when a strike makes contact with a target.

OBLIGATORY STANDARDS: the concept and belief that having capabilities requires the individual possessing them to use them simply because the individual has the capabilities.

PECTORALIS MUSCLES: the muscles of the chest.

POSITIVE IMPACT FORCE: the measure of striking power yielded from a blow which affects the target.

POSITIVE MOTION: forward or progressive movement.

POSTURE GROUP: muscles of the body which maintain the body in an upright or other selected position.

POSTURE OF A WEAPON: the manner in which the joints are bent, turned or held rigid to form an anatomical weapon.

SYNCHRONIZATION: properly timed; to occur at a prescribed rate.

SYNTAX: systematic; arranged; orderly.

TENDONS: connective tissues which bind muscles to bones.

TORSO: the main trunk of the body: chest, abdomen, etc.

TOTAL IMPACT FORCE: the sum of contact with a target.

TRAJECTORY: path of a moving object.

TRICEPS: muscles of the rear upper portion of the arm.

ULNA: longer of the two bones of the forearm.

VELOCITY: rate of motion; speed.

VERTICAL: up and down; top to bottom.